HEARD ACKNOWLEDGED NOTICED NOTEWORTHY AMPLIFIED

HANNA

ADRIANA LUNA CARLOS
Editor-In-Chief, Designer
and Co-Founder

HANNA OLIVAS
Managing Editor &
Co-Founder

NICOLE CURTIS
Director of the SRS
Magazine Division

ADVERTISING OPPORTUNITIES

Info@SheRisesStudios.com

HANNA MAGAZINE
MAY 2025

SHE RISES STUDIOS

CONTACT US

SheRisesStudios@gmail.com

WWW.SHERISESSTUDIOS.COM

LETTER FROM THE **EDITORS**

Dear Reader,

Welcome to the May 2025 edition of HANNA Magazine, a powerful celebration of the voices that break barriers, ignite transformation, and pave the way for a more inclusive and empowered world. This month's theme, Voices Of Impact: Elevating Stories That Matter, calls us to listen more deeply, speak more boldly, and honor the courage it takes to rise, share, and lead.

Our cover feature, Nikki Hillhouse, is a stroke-thriver, transformational coach, and beacon of resilience whose journey from chronic pain to powerful purpose is a testament to radical self-belief and unshakable faith. As a Holistic Wellness Expert, Wellness Retreat Facilitator and soon-to-be author, Nikki embodies her mission to help others alchemize adversity into light. Through her holistic approach, she amplifies the quiet whispers of intuition, heals the wounds we carry in silence, and reminds us that we are worthy, capable, and powerful beyond measure.

Through this edition, we spotlight changemakers like Nikki who are rewriting narratives, advocating for wellness, justice, equity, and inner peace, and using their platforms to lift others. From holistic healing to fierce advocacy, these stories are the heartbeat of HANNA—a magazine where every voice matters and every story deserves the mic.
Thank you for joining us in this celebration of transformation and truth. May this issue inspire you to share your story, own your voice, and believe—just like Nikki does—that all things are possible.

Warm regards,

Adriana Luna Carlos, Hanna Olivas and Nicole Curtis
Editors of HANNA Magazine

SHE WINS
GLOBAL SUMMIT 2025

This is more than an event—it's a movement!

Join 500+ unstoppable women for two days of powerful keynotes, celebrity fireside chats, business growth strategies, and high-level networking. Elevate your career, expand your influence, and connect with industry leaders shaping the future!

Want To Take The Stage!

We're inviting dynamic speakers to share expertise on finance, leadership, branding, health, tech, and more! Elevate your voice, gain global exposure on FENIX TV, and unlock Exclusive Speaker Perks worth over $2,000!

Apply to Speak Today!

 https://form.jotform.com/250646617740156

NOVEMBER 6-7 2025 | LAS VEGAS, NEVADA

UNLOCKING A LIFE WITHOUT LIMITS:

Nikki Hillhouse's Journey to Healing and Empowerment

In a world where adversity often dictates the narrative of our lives, some individuals choose to rewrite their story, defying expectations and proving that transformation is not only possible but inevitable when approached with resilience and self-belief. Nikki is one such individual—a woman whose journey from chronic pain and struggle to radiant health and empowerment is nothing short of remarkable. As a Mind Detox Practitioner, Meditation Teacher, Well-being Coach, International Speaker, Wellness Retreat Facilitator, and soon-to-be author, she has dedicated her life to helping others heal, transform, and unlock their full potential.

A Journey Born from Personal Struggles

For Nikki, the path to holistic health was not merely a career choice but a necessity. After facing significant health challenges, she found herself at a crossroads—one where conventional medicine offered only limited relief. It was then that she embarked on a deeply personal quest to reclaim her well-being, exploring alternative healing methods that addressed not just the body but also the mind and soul. Through meditation, energy healing, and holistic therapies, she discovered a profound truth: true healing is not about treating symptoms but about addressing the root causes of distress. This realization became the foundation of her life's work.

The Power of Possibility

"All Things Are Possible." This is not just a mantra for Nikki—it's a belief system she has lived by, especially during her most challenging times.

One of the most defining moments in her life was her recovery from a stroke. Doctors painted a bleak prognosis, insisting that a full recovery was unlikely. But Nikki refused to accept limitations imposed upon her. Instead, she turned inward, asking herself, *"What if they're wrong?"* That question became the catalyst for her healing. She understood that healing wasn't just about the physical—it was about restoring balance within her mind, heart, body, and soul. By embodying her belief in limitless possibilities, she defied expectations and proved that the human spirit is far more powerful than any diagnosis.

Breaking Barriers: Helping Others Overcome Their Blocks
Through her work as a Mind Detox Practitioner and Well-being Coach, Nikki has encountered many individuals struggling with common blocks that hinder their growth. Limiting beliefs, unresolved emotional trauma, fear of change, self-doubt, and chronic stress are just a few of the obstacles she helps clients overcome. Her approach is rooted in transformation—helping people identify and release negative patterns while replacing them with empowering beliefs. Through meditation, energy healing, and mindset shifts, she equips individuals with the tools they need to break free from the barriers holding them back.

A Voice for Healing: The Upcoming Book
Soon, Nikki will add *"author"* to her impressive list of accomplishments. Her upcoming book is a teaching memoir—a blend of personal experiences and transformative tools that guide readers toward healing and self-discovery. By sharing her own journey, she aims to inspire others to heal emotional wounds, release past traumas, and reconnect with their authentic selves. Her book is not just about telling a story; it's about offering a roadmap to a life without limits.

Additionally, Nikki has contributed chapters to two separate anthologies for She Rises Studios, further amplifying her message of resilience and empowerment. These collaborations allow her to reach a broader audience, proving that adversity can be transformed into a powerful force for growth.

A Sanctuary for Transformation: Wellness Retreats in Turkey
Set against the breathtaking backdrop of Turkey's serene landscapes, Nikki's wellness retreats offer more than just relaxation—they provide a sanctuary for deep transformation. What makes these retreats unique is the holistic approach she curates, combining meditation, yoga, energy healing, and Mind Detox techniques. Attendees leave with more than just a sense of calm; they experience profound shifts in self-awareness, clarity, and empowerment. These retreats serve as a reminder that healing is not a destination but a journey—one that is best undertaken with intention and support.

Reconnecting with Intuition: A Path to Self-Discovery
One of the greatest challenges people face is the disconnection from their intuition—their inner wisdom that often gets drowned out by external noise and self-doubt. Nikki teaches that reconnecting with intuition requires stillness and trust. Simple yet powerful practices like mindful breathing, meditation, and journaling can help individuals tune in to their inner voice. According to her, the body holds wisdom, communicating through physical sensations and emotions. By listening closely and creating space for reflection, anyone can cultivate a stronger connection with their intuition.

Mindset Shifts for Lasting Change
Nikki knows firsthand that overcoming adversity is not just about external actions but internal transformations. Shifting from a victim mentality to a survivor's mindset was crucial in her own healing.

She learned to ask herself, *"What perspective am I choosing today?"* This self-awareness allowed her to reclaim her power, embrace self-compassion, and trust in the possibility of transformation. By focusing on presence, acceptance, and self-kindness, she turned pain into purpose and challenges into opportunities for growth.

A Holistic Approach to Coaching

What sets Nikki apart as a healer and coach is her integrative approach. She combines coaching, therapy, and meditation to facilitate deep healing. Through techniques like Calm Cure and Mind Detox, she helps clients release emotional baggage and limiting beliefs, making space for renewed clarity and confidence. Her sessions provide a safe and compassionate space where individuals feel truly seen, heard, and empowered to take control of their own healing journey.

A Simple Yet Powerful Practice for Beginners

For those just beginning their journey of self-discovery, Nikki suggests starting with something simple yet profound—mindful breathing. A few minutes of focused breathing each day can create space for awareness, reduce stress, and cultivate resilience. By inhaling deeply, holding for a moment, and exhaling slowly, individuals can anchor themselves in the present and develop a stronger connection with their inner selves.

What's Next for Nikki?

As Nikki continues her mission to empower others, exciting new projects lie ahead. With the upcoming release of her book, expanded wellness retreats, and more speaking engagements, she is set to reach and inspire even more people around the world. Writing for magazines, collaborating with like-minded healers, and creating new initiatives focused on healing and empowerment are all part of her evolving vision. Her commitment remains steadfast: to help individuals rewrite their stories, embrace their worth, and live a life without limits.

Living Without Limits

Nikki's journey is a testament to the power of resilience, belief, and transformation. From overcoming personal adversity to guiding others toward healing, she embodies the truth that all things are possible. Through her work, she continues to inspire others to step into their power, reconnect with their intuition, and create lives filled with freedom, fulfillment, and purpose. In a world often clouded by doubt and fear, Nikki stands as a beacon of hope, reminding us all that healing is within reach and that we are far more powerful than we realize.

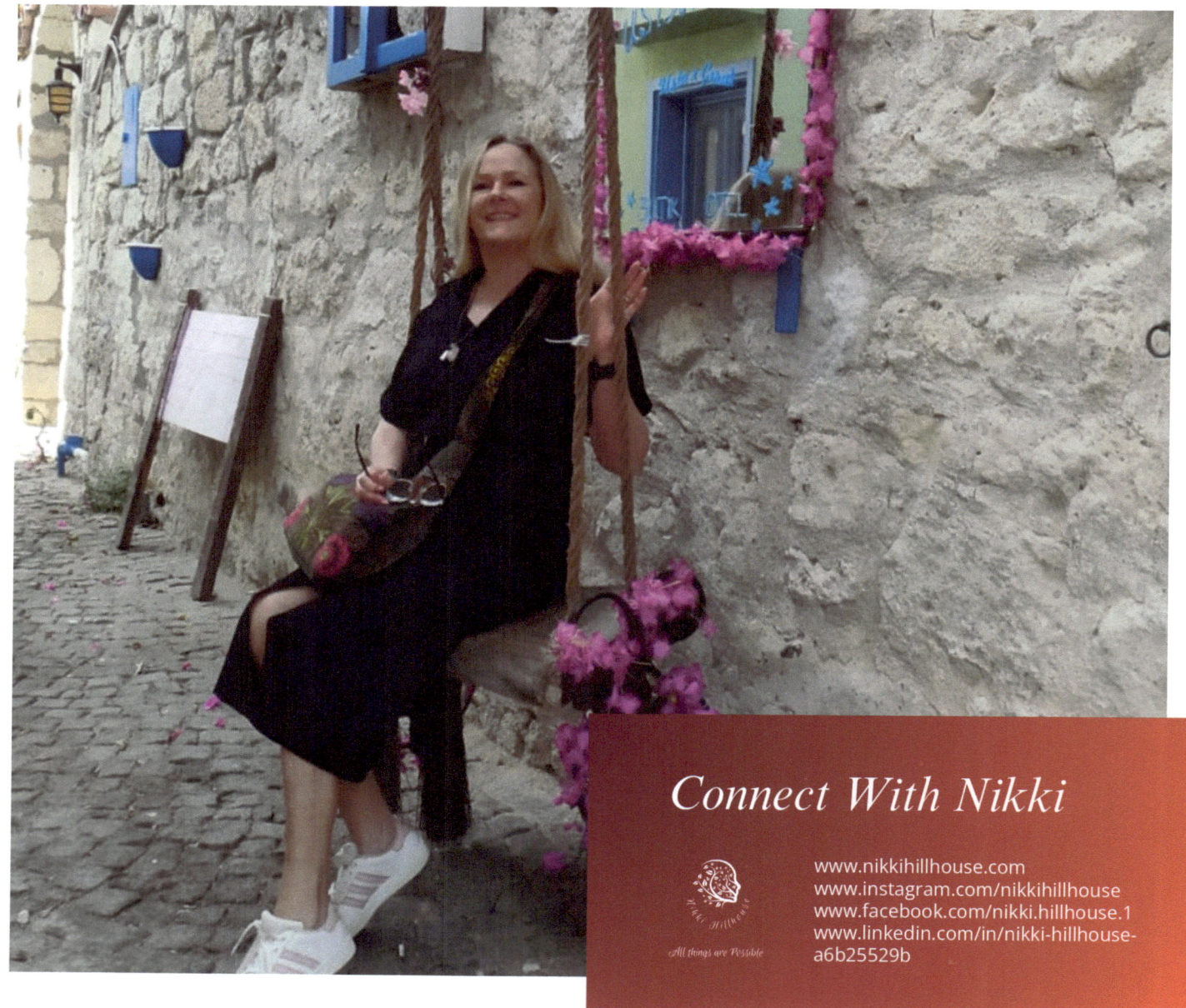

Connect With Nikki

All things are Possible

www.nikkihillhouse.com
www.instagram.com/nikkihillhouse
www.facebook.com/nikki.hillhouse.1
www.linkedin.com/in/nikki-hillhouse-a6b25529b

THE UNSTOPPABLE SPARK:
A Journey of Resilience and Bold Transformation

By Lovely LaGuerre

Life, as we know it, is a tapestry of moments each one an opportunity to define who we are and who we're meant to become. My story is not simply one of triumph, but of resilience, reinvention, and the audacious pursuit of beauty in every twist and turn life has to offer. It's a story that invites you to pause, reflect, and ultimately rise, unapologetically owning your unique brilliance.

My path was not paved with certainty, nor was it void of trials. It was shaped by moments of doubt, struggle, and transformation. I have faced the kind of challenges that demand not just endurance but the courage to rewrite story when life writes an unexpected chapter. These were not just moments of survival they were catalysts for a deeper kind of strength, one rooted in purpose and vision.

Every hurdle I encountered became a stepping stone, each setback an invitation to uncover layers of untapped potential. What could have broken me became the very foundation for a life marked by intention and reinvention. I learned that the greatest stories often emerge not from the smoothest journeys, but from the resilience shown in navigating the roughest seas.

Moreover, resilience alone isn't enough it must be paired with vision. Mine was clear: to transform not only my life but also to empower others to do the same. I envisioned creating something meaningful, something that would inspire others to look beyond their circumstances and embrace their inherent ability to thrive.

Through dedication, faith, and sheer determination, I transformed my vision into reality. With every step forward, I knew I wasn't just building a business or a brand I was building a legacy of empowerment. Each product, service, and initiative I've created carries the essence of my journey, a testament to what is possible when we refuse to let challenges define us.

My inspiration stems from the belief that beauty isn't just a physical expression it's a reflection of the strength, confidence, and joy that comes from embracing your true self. I've built this foundation on the principle that we all deserve to feel beautiful, valued, and celebrated, no matter where we come from or what we've endured.

Today, I stand as proof that resilience paired with boldness can change lives. My story is a reminder that you are never too broken, too lost, or too defeated to rise again. If there's one truth I hope to impart, it's this: Your story is your power. It is uniquely yours to own, shape, and share with the world.

I invite you to step into your own narrative with courage and authenticity. Let your experiences both the triumphs and the trials become the foundation for something extraordinary. Embrace change, rise above doubt, and brew something beautiful out of life's most unexpected moments.

The time to live boldly and unapologetically is now. Your journey is your masterpiece, and the world is waiting for your spark.

Connect With Lovely

www.pureheavenlyhair.com
www.lovelysellsvegas.com
www.instagram.com/pureheavenlyhair
www.twitter.com/Heavenly_Pure
www.facebook.com/share/1Bau9f8Ld6
www.in.pinterest.com/pureheavenly/wig-products

SHIFTING THE GLOBAL MINDSET:

A Vision for a More Unified, Compassionate World

By Maaria Mozaffar

We are more alike than we are different

We have a blood pumping heart, muscles that move us and bones that hold us.

When we lose a limb, we feel devastated and defeated.

We were born through our mothers and hold our babies till they fall asleep.

We are in pain when we are hungry and cold when we are without shelter. Our skin feels frostbite and sunburn and if we walked miles without shoes our feet would be sting with blisters.

We have values that transcend identity

We want our children to feel safe at night. We want our children to feel they can depend on our words when we say *"It will be alright".*

We want our parents to feel protected in their old age.

We want our partners to come home to us at night and safely reach their destinations when they travel without us. We value family. We value safety, We value rest when needed. We value the duty to protect and the right to be protected.

Policies have to be seen as human first

Legislations passed by the legislature are created to solve problems. With the foundations of efficiency and equity being the ideals of their success. We create these policies to create systems and processes that provide balance in our communities. Then how is it that efficient systems result so often in negative human impact? For example, why is it that we don't connect the dots between poor determinants of health to food deserts, poor public education or access to health services? If we are to solve problems, what about the people that we are solving them for? In my work I have too often seen the target of policies to be one that focuses on efficiency of a community while seeing people as a liability. If we fail to see policies as a method to have fairness and mercy on the humans and its impacts, we will be creating systems that only further harm the people the policies are aimed to protect. Efficiency cannot be traded for human dignity.

Empathy is the superpower

By recognizing how another life can be improved by seeing myself in their shoes, we are able to get closer to a solution we are attempting to advance in a variety of societal issues. I have found this exercise in my legislative work to be extremely powerful, humbling.

We cannot adequately gather information on the harm that needs to be alleviated unless we can see how the harm would impact us as human beings ourselves.

Technology can be used to divide us or unite us

Despite the access to technology which could provide windows to the world, we are creating self serving echo chambers that divide us based on the perceptions we adopt about other communities. The more we believe and internalize these perceptions, the more we create algorithms that cement our opinions. Thus deliberately, we are choosing to amplify our differences and see less humanity in one another.

Discrimination, Ethnocentrism, Racism is a learned behavior.

I wish I could say that some people are just born with a desire to divide or create unjust systems for others. It would be a lot easier to understand the lack of a desire for some to unite on overarching ideals and suffering. Yet, these notions are learned. They are adopted by consistently seeing global suffering and harm even at the local level so often, that for some it becomes part of the natural order of our world. We don't have to accept that. Empathy is just as natural as apathy. Human dignity is just as vital as efficiency.

Connect With Maaria

www.maariamozaffar.com
www.instagram.com/mozaffarmaaria
www.linkedin.com/in/maaria-mozaffar

GET YOUR COPY NOW

Celebrate the power of women through inspiring stories and insights.

How I Unlearned My Crap
Kathy Baldwin

Stepping Up to Lead
Annabelle and India Beckwith

Redefined Flourishing In
Life While Becoming Wife
Breanna James

Redefining You
Amanda Cahill

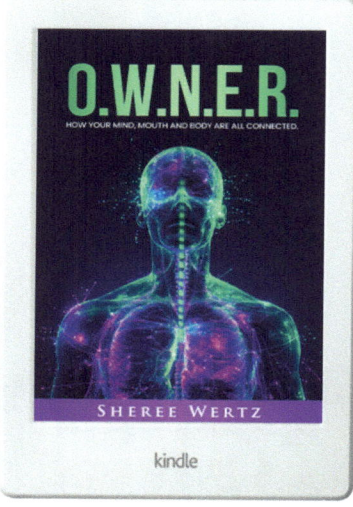

O.W.N.E.R.
Sheree Wertz

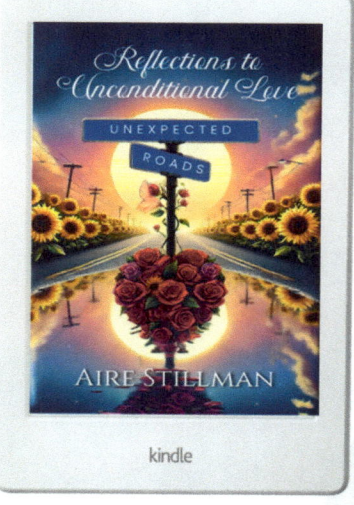

Reflections to Unconditional Love
Aire Stillman

FENIX TV

YOUR PLATFORM, YOUR VOICE, YOUR POWER!

Step into the Spotlight as a Host on FENIX TV!

Are you ready to amplify your message, inspire others, and be part of a groundbreaking network dedicated to **empowering women worldwide**? FENIX TV is your platform to **shine as a host**, share your expertise, and connect with a global audience.

WHY HOST ON FENIX TV?

- Reach a worldwide audience passionate about empowerment
- Showcase your voice, brand, and expertise
- Join a community of inspiring leaders and changemakers
- Be part of a network that uplifts and celebrates women

Whether you dream of leading a talk show, sharing powerful stories, or educating and inspiring others—FENIX TV is where your voice matters!

SPOTS ARE LIMITED! Secure your hosting opportunity today.

 Contact us now at
info@fenixtv.app

 Learn more at
https://fenixtv.app

BREAKING BARRIERS:

Nyle DiMarco's Journey to Amplify Deaf Culture and Inclusion

When you think of trailblazers who have turned challenges into platforms for change, Nyle DiMarco stands as an emblem of resilience, advocacy, and empowerment. A deaf model, actor, and activist, DiMarco has not only redefined success but has also shattered societal stigmas surrounding the deaf community. Through his remarkable journey and unwavering commitment to accessibility and inclusion, he continues to inspire millions worldwide.

Early Life and Embracing Deaf Identity

Born into a multigenerational deaf family, Nyle DiMarco grew up immersed in a rich culture of sign language and communication. With American Sign Language (ASL) as his first language, he navigated a world that often marginalized his community, but his upbringing instilled a deep sense of pride in his identity.

DiMarco's early experiences highlighted the barriers faced by the deaf community, from educational disparities to societal misconceptions. Despite these challenges, he refused to let his deafness define his potential. Instead, he embraced it as a unique strength and a source of empowerment.

Rising to Stardom

Nyle's rise to fame began when he became the first deaf winner of *"America's Next Top Model"* in 2015. His win was a historic moment, showcasing that talent transcends traditional communication barriers. He followed this victory with another groundbreaking achievement: winning *"Dancing with the Stars"* in 2016. On the dance floor, he captivated audiences with his ability to convey emotion and rhythm through movement—proving that the language of expression is universal.

While his accomplishments in the entertainment industry brought him widespread recognition, DiMarco used his platform for a purpose far greater than personal fame. His success became a megaphone to amplify the voices of the deaf community and advocate for systemic change.

Advocacy Through the Nyle DiMarco Foundation

In 2016, DiMarco founded the Nyle DiMarco Foundation, a nonprofit organization dedicated to improving the lives of deaf individuals. The foundation focuses on promoting early access to language acquisition, which is critical for cognitive and social development. Statistics show that 90% of deaf children are born to hearing parents, many of whom lack the resources or knowledge to teach their children sign language. This language deprivation can lead to long-term developmental delays.

DiMarco's foundation works tirelessly to bridge this gap by providing educational resources, advocating for bilingual education in ASL and English, and raising awareness about the importance of early intervention. By addressing these systemic issues, the foundation empowers deaf individuals to thrive in a world that often overlooks their needs.

Challenging Stigmas and Celebrating Deaf Culture
One of DiMarco's most significant contributions is his role in normalizing deafness and celebrating deaf culture. He frequently challenges misconceptions about what it means to be deaf, emphasizing that it is not a disability but a cultural identity. Through social media, public speaking, and his memoir Deaf Utopia, DiMarco shares stories of resilience and joy within the deaf community, fostering greater understanding and acceptance.

His activism also extends to the entertainment industry. As an actor and producer, DiMarco advocates for authentic representation of deaf characters and storylines in film and television. He has worked on projects like Netflix's Deaf U, a reality series that provides an unfiltered look into the lives of deaf college students, and the Oscar-winning film CODA, which centers on a hearing child of deaf adults. These works not only amplify deaf voices but also challenge Hollywood to prioritize inclusivity and authenticity.

> *"Own your identity. Love who you are in the world. Love your deafness."*

A Vision for an Inclusive Future
Beyond his individual achievements, Nyle DiMarco's impact lies in his vision for a more inclusive society. He believes that accessibility is a fundamental right, not a privilege, and advocates for systemic changes that benefit all individuals with disabilities. From pushing for captions on social media platforms to promoting universal design principles, DiMarco's efforts extend beyond the deaf community to create a world that values diversity and inclusion.

Nyle DiMarco's story is a powerful reminder of the value of being heard—in every sense of the word. By challenging stigmas, celebrating deaf culture, and advocating for inclusion, DiMarco has become a beacon of hope and a catalyst for progress. As we honor National Speech and Hearing Awareness Month, let us celebrate trailblazers like Nyle DiMarco who remind us that true empowerment lies in breaking barriers, fostering understanding, and creating a world where everyone's voice can be heard.

When the *Shame* is *Louder* Than the *Strategy*

By Jacqueline Crider

The untold side of financial freedom—and why doing it *"right"* doesn't always feel right.

You followed the rules. Paid off the debt. Built the savings. Created the budget. And still—some nights, you lie awake wondering if it could all vanish. What if you're not doing enough? What if it's too late to get it together? What if —despite everything—you're just not cut out for this?

I know that feeling. Because I've lived it —deeply.

I grew up in a house where money was talked about. My mom made me read Sound Mind Investing in seventh grade. I understood the mechanics. I learned to save, to plan, to hustle. But the truth? I still didn't trust myself with money.

That lack of trust shaped everything. I gave up financial control in my first marriage because I believed my impulse to spend made me unfit to manage money. That decision—rooted in shame—led to financial abuse. And when the marriage ended, the chaos didn't stop. It escalated.

I spiraled. Broke my own budget. Racked up debt. Operated in survival mode.

And here's the part most financial advice never covers: The problem wasn't my budget. It was my biology.

Most of us weren't taught to trust ourselves with money—we were taught to fear it. We grew up with tight grocery lists, whispered arguments over bills, or guilt around asking for more. And so, even when things look *"better"* on the outside... the fear stays.

Because your body isn't wired for wealth. It's wired for safety.

If your nervous system is still operating from a place of survival, then no raise, no savings goal, no spreadsheet will ever make you feel secure.

I had to unlearn that. And just in time—because life tested it.

My daughter was born eight weeks early. We spent 47 days in the NICU. Right after, my business was blindsided—we were dropped from our brokerage, lost our pipeline, and took a 30% pay cut. Then the market turned. And then—our dream home, under contract to sell, flooded from a faucet left running for days. Over $300,000 in damages.

Ten years ago? That would've wrecked me. But I didn't spiral. I didn't freeze. Why?

Because I had done the work. I had reset my nervous system. I had learned to trust myself.

Financial freedom isn't a number in your bank account. It's how calm you stay when the numbers drop, when things go wrong.

If you've ever thought:
"Maybe I'm just not built for financial success."
"At my age, I shouldn't still be struggling with this."
"If people knew how bad it got... they'd judge me."

Let me tell you right now:
- That voice isn't your truth. It's your trauma.
- You are not your balance sheet.
- You are not your past.
- You are not broken—you are rewiring.

You don't need to budget harder. You need to breathe deeper.
You don't need another *"rulebook."* You need self-trust.
You don't need to earn peace. You get to choose it.

A Gentle Step Forward
If your nervous system is tired of the hustle—
If your mind is begging for calm around money—
The Aligned Action Planner might be the soft reset you've been needing.

It's 14 days of thoughtful, no-pressure prompts designed to bring your financial world back into focus—with clarity, peace, and choice at the center.

No shame. No overwhelm. Just small aligned actions that feel like you.

Because your story isn't over. And this next chapter? It gets to feel different.

Scan the QR Code to learn more.

Connect With Us

www.urals.co/jax-crider
www.facebook.com/jax.crider
www.instagram.com/jax_crider
www.linkedin.com/in/pbj-mortgage-jacqueline-crider

BIRTHING
Season

By Tiffany Tyler-Garner, PhD

This month, we celebrate Mother's Day, a celebration acknowledging our ability to birth and nurture. As we celebrate this acknowledgement, we have an opportunity to consider what we may birth should we acknowledge that we each have the ability to bring something into the world through our talents, gifts and strengths. Moreover, this ability is not relegated to the ability to physically birth life. Rather, we are all positioned to birth a new season, mindset, opportunity, or change.

We all possess the ability to birth spiritually, financially, emotionally and mentally. These abilities are not contingent on gender, age or mating. Should we decide, we can birth throughout our lives, with varying gestational periods. We can have multiple births and deliveries. We have an opportunity to birth something new each day.

We are only limited by our imagination.

However, there are some ways in which our birthing will be like a physical pregnancy.

We should be prepared to eat right and rest if we are to sustain our efforts. We must create space in our lives to cultivate the things we hope to raise. Like a nursery, we must make space for the activities that will be required to fully realize our results.

We must know that as our vision, new practice, mindset or investments grow, we will experience periods of discomfort. Like Braxton Hicks contractions, we may encounter false labor or fear things are happening too soon. In both of these instances, our work is to remember what will be gained and our birthing plan.

Like a physical pregnancy, we will swell in expected ways and unexpected ways. We will grow as our vision, mindset, practice or investment grows.

There will be times when we wonder if we physically have the capacity to continue growing and carrying what we hope to birth. This is a sign that we are getting closer to realizing what we desire.

As we come closer to realizing our new season, chapter, mindset, or innovation, we will begin to crown. We will begin to see what we are birthing come to fruition. It is important to note that this might feel painful.

Our work during this time is to bear down and push. If we do not, it could die, we could die, or it may be the death of both the thing we were to give to the world and who we were to become.

This is the time to lean on the midwives, doulas and significant others in your life.

Hopefully you have surrounded yourself with people you can trust, who will hold your hand, and tell you to breath—breath as you deliver your dreams!

In support of this glorious ability, the ability birth, I ask you to consider what you might birth if you renewed your focus, set intention, and continued the work of delivering your dreams!

Happy birthing season!

Connect With Tiffany

@drtgtyler on Instagram
@drtgtyler on Facebook
www.linkedin.com/in/dr-tiffany-tyler-garner-a603431b
www.drtylerinspires.com

JEN RIGLEY

Speaker, Author, Founder of Flourishing Over Fifty® and creator of The Flourish Journey™

It's May....and Spring has sprung here in Chicago. It's time for renewal as we shed the chill of winter and move into rain showers and rainbows. I like to think of it as a grand re-awakening which makes it the perfect time to do some Spring cleaning.

This isn't the type of Spring cleaning that comes most immediately to mind like cleaning out the closets. This is a life journey Spring cleaning. This grand re-awakening is the perfect time to delve into how life is treating you and how you are showing up for life.

I have the perfect tool for this Spring cleaning project. It's an activity that I lead in my workshops based on The Flourish Journey™, a transformative seven-step framework I designed specifically to help women like you reclaim the life you deserve.

The Perfect Day

Can you envision your perfect day? Close your eyes and take a few minutes to begin dreaming about how your perfect day unfolds. Allow yourself to be fully present, connecting deeply to each of your senses, and feel what resonates with you.

SIGHT What does your perfect day look like? Do you see yourself at the beach, in your cozy home, on a mountain top, or surrounded by your loved ones?

TOUCH What does your perfect day feel like? Can you feel the hot sand on your feet, that perfect soft blanket on your legs, the breeze as you approach the top of the mountain, or those special hugs from your kids?

SOUND What does your perfect day sound like? Can you hear the soothing rhythm of waves slowly rolling on the shore, your favorite melody playing softly, the quietness atop a mountain, or the joyful laughter of family?

TASTE What does your perfect day taste like? Do you feel the icy coolness of a popsicle, the savory flavor of your special homemade bread, the smooth, sweet richness of a peanut butter and jelly sandwich eaten after reaching the peak, or the crunch of a bowl of popcorn shared with all?

SMELL What aromas surround you on this perfect day? Can you breathe in that special mix of sand and sea, the scent of your favorite candle, the pine needles from the towering trees along your hike, or the many scents made up of each of your children?

How beautiful is it that we can summon all of our senses to envision our perfect life?

By envisioning your perfect day using all of your senses you'll gain profound clarity, empowering yourself to nurture what uplifts you and lovingly release what no longer serves you.

This is the perfect activity to inspire you to create a new story for your life. Join the Flourishing Over Fifty® community and reclaim your joy, rewrite your story, and flourish—together.

Scan the QR code or follow the link to join our community, receive a free gift and take your first step towards the life you truly deserve.

Connect With Jen

www.bit.ly/hannaselfcare
www.facebook.com/flourishingoverfifty
www.instagram.com/flourishingoverfifty

The SHE RISES STUDIOS PODCAST

TUNE IN. RISE UP. THRIVE.

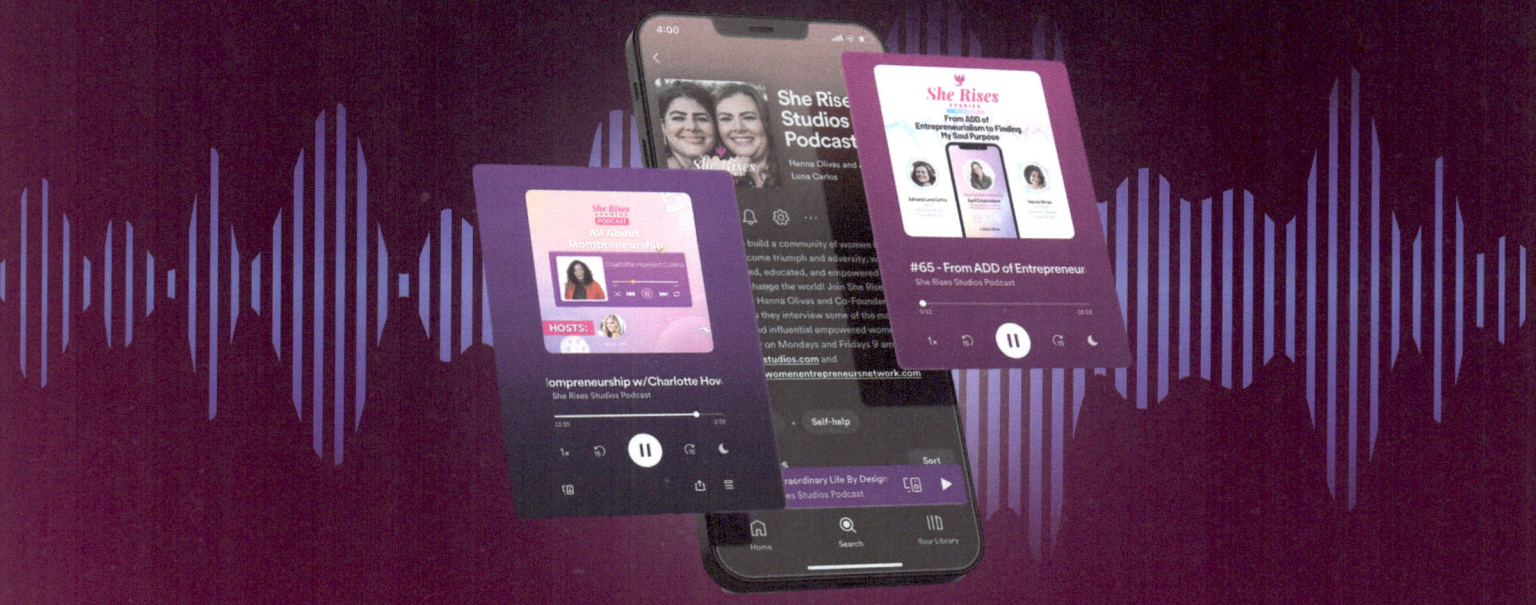

Looking for **real conversations** that inspire, empower, and ignite your potential? The **SRS Podcast** is where women like you come to **learn, grow, and rise!**

Join us for powerful **interviews with trailblazing entrepreneurs, thought leaders, and everyday women** who have turned obstacles into opportunities. Our episodes dive into:

- **Breaking through self-doubt** and stepping into confidence
- **Building a thriving business** with purpose and passion
- **Mastering work-life balance** without guilt
- **Leveling up your mindset, health, and career**
- **Finding your true purpose and living boldly**

Each episode is packed with **real stories, expert insights, and actionable strategies** to help you take your life to the next level. **This isn't just a podcast—it's your roadmap to success!**

SUBSCRIBE NOW AND START YOUR JOURNEY TO EMPOWERMENT!

GET YOUR COPY NOW

Celebrate the power of women through inspiring stories and insights.

From Surviving to Thriving
Gina Stockdall

Shifting Narratives
Anita Comisky and Michelle Belloit

Stepping into Wadzi:
Lessons from my life
Wadzanai Garwe

Garden to Kitchen Planner
Ines Batterton

Invisible to Visible
Julie Lavia

Unlearn the Crap and Level Up
Kathy Baldwin

EMBRACING SOLITUDE:

A Journey to Self-Love and Connection

By DK Hillard

We've all heard these words so many times: *"You must learn to love yourself."* And yet, for many of us, they can feel almost impossible to truly grasp. I know this because I've heard them over and over throughout my life, only to dismiss them each time. I believed that there had to be something grander in store for me, something beyond the simplicity of *"self-love."* That was my ego speaking, not my soul.

Now, in my seventh decade, those words have finally started to sink in. Learning to love yourself is a journey we all must take in our own way. It's a truth many of us may resist, but it's one we cannot escape. Trauma survivors, in particular, are often hard-wired to look outside of themselves, believing that there is someone or something out there better than we are. We are taught to think we don't know what we know, that the answers lie outside of us, but time and time again, I've found that the truth, the answers to nearly every challenge I've faced, have always been within me.

I recall a time nearly 20 years ago, when I was alone in a hotel room in San Francisco. My husband was away on business, and I wasn't feeling well enough to go out. I found myself deeply reflecting and, as I often do, I went to the mirror and looked into my own eyes. It was a simple act, one I had done countless times before—both for myself and with clients when I was a coach. But this time, I was in a different state of being and what I saw in the mirror took me by surprise. It was as if I had traveled back through time. My eyes spoke to me, showing me glimpses of who I was, of everything I had lived through. I saw pain, yes, but also wisdom beyond measure. In those eyes, I saw both the deepest darkness and the brightest light imaginable. And in that moment, I knew who I was. I bridged the gap between worlds, outside of time and space, and saw my soul staring back at me. It was a moment I will never forget.

This is what I mean when I talk about self-love. It's about being with myself, alone yet connected, seeing the truth of who I am and learning to love all that I see. My strength and frailties. My wisdom and ignorance. My beauty and my flaws. Self-love must come first before anything else can fall into place. By honoring all that I am—and all that I am not—I no longer have to run from myself. I have found a home in my own skin. I no longer judge or condemn myself. Instead, I turn to myself for the wisdom I seek and the answers I need. I trust myself above all others, and I honor what I need and desire as if I were loving the most precious being on earth.

Solitude opens the space for me to commune with my soul and the spirits that guide me, allowing me to strengthen those relationships. It provides me with the opportunity to hold my own hand through this journey called life.

If you take anything from my story, let it be this: self-love is not a destination but a practice—a daily choice to honor who you are. The more you cultivate it, the more you'll find peace in your own skin and guidance in your own heart. And remember, you are never truly alone.

Connect With DK

www.facebook.com/dkhillardwraptures
www.linkedin.com/in/debra-hillard-93526913
www.instagram.com/dkhillard
www.dkhillard.com
www.dkhillardart.com

BUILDING A *LEGACY*

By Idaliz Romero

I made the decision to retire earlier than planned due to a family illness. In the midst of navigating that difficult time, I quickly realized that survivor benefits weren't enough to sustain even the most basic necessities. The financial strain left me searching for something more—an opportunity to rebuild, to create security, and to regain a sense of purpose.

I explored many options, but nothing truly spoke to me. Then, in the midst of my search, I discovered my love for writing. It became my outlet: A way to share my journey, my struggles, and my triumphs. Through this passion, I was fortunate to collaborate with incredible authors, contributing to four anthologies, two of which became international bestsellers. Writing became a source of healing, opening doors I never imagined.

As I connected with inspiring individuals—entrepreneurs, visionaries, and those dedicated to making a difference—I realized that I wanted more than just an income. I wanted a life filled with purpose, service, and impact.

Then, someone introduced me to a travel business opportunity, and something inside me lit up. I attended a presentation, and for the first time in a long time, I felt like I had found exactly what I had been searching for. The timing, however, wasn't perfect. My finances were tight, and even though I wanted to say an enthusiastic YES, I hesitated. Month after month, I had to decline. But the opportunity stayed in my heart.

Then one day, I made the decision. No more waiting. No more letting fear or finances dictate my future. I took a leap of faith, knowing that this was an investment in myself, my dreams, and the legacy I wanted to create. And I'm so grateful I did. Within my first few months, I completed certain travel certifications and, most importantly, found a community that truly supports and uplifts one another.

From the moment I joined, I was welcomed into a community that uplifted and supported me. I learned about the world of travel, the incredible perks, and the life-changing experiences that come with it. And as I embraced this new journey, one thought stood out above all—I wanted to create lasting memories for my granddaughters. The idea of showing them the world, one destination at a time, ignited a passion in me like never before.

Now, I am building a travel business focused on helping grandparents create unforgettable experiences with their grandchildren—memories that will be cherished for a lifetime. This business isn't just about travel; it's about relationships, adventure, and the freedom to design life on your own terms. It's about earning while exploring the world and, most importantly, leaving a financial legacy for future generations. The opportunity to build something meaningful, to work from anywhere, and to help others create lifelong memories is truly priceless.

What would you do if you had the freedom to work from anywhere? Where would you go first?

Imagine being the person who helps others experience the magic of seeing the world. Imagine building a future where you have the freedom to work on your own terms, to create wealth, and to leave something behind for those you love.

If you've been looking for something more, if you've been waiting for a sign—this is it. Get in touch and let me show you how you can do this too.

Take the leap. Build the legacy. Create the memories. Let's explore this opportunity together!!

Connect With Idaliz

www.linkedin.com/in/idalizromero
www.facebook.com/idaliz.romero
www.instagram.com/lizzyret3

EMPOWERED VOICES:

Leading Boldly with Authenticity

By Carol Salvadori

Have you ever felt the pressure to conform in order to succeed? In a world where voices can easily get lost amidst a sea of sameness, authentic leadership is not simply a choice—it's a necessity. The journey to finding and embracing our true selves is a powerful one, capable of not only transforming our own paths but also inspiring those around us.

As the founder of LEADLoud Academy, my journey began with a profound realization: true impact comes from being boldly authentic. There was a time when I navigated complex professional landscapes, trying to fit into moulds that were never designed for me. It was only when I started to listen to my inner voice that I began to understand the true meaning of leadership. Embracing my real self allowed me to connect on a deeper level with those around me, building trust and fostering collaboration.

Authenticity in leadership is crucial for several reasons. Firstly, it builds a foundation of trust. When leaders are transparent and genuine, they create an environment where team members feel seen and valued. This, in turn, enhances engagement and performance. Secondly, authentic leaders inspire creativity and innovation by encouraging others to bring their true selves to the table. A diverse mix of perspectives leads to rich ideas that drive success.

But how can you start embracing authenticity in your leadership journey? It begins with self-reflection. Take time to understand your values, strengths, and areas you're passionate about. Create a vision for how you want to show up as a leader and align your actions with these core beliefs. Secondly, practice active listening—not just to those around you, but also to your inner voice. It will guide you toward decisions and actions that resonate with your true self.

LEADLoud Academy is dedicated to supporting individuals on this path. We believe that each leader's unique voice is their most powerful tool. Our programs are designed to amplify these voices, providing the skills and confidence needed to lead with authenticity and impact. Through a blend of mentorship, community, and innovative methodologies, we empower leaders to stand out and thrive.

You possess a voice that is both unique and powerful. Embrace it, nurture it, and watch as it transforms not only your leadership but the world around you. At LEADLoud Academy, we believe that when leaders speak authentically, they ignite change. So step forward with confidence and let your true voice shine—because bold leaders with authentic voices are the ones who truly win.

Connect With Carol

www.linkedin.com/in/leadloudacademy
Free E-Book: www.leadloudacademy.mykajabi.com/opt-in-d401b2c7-5292-4dba-9924-1f8912dd064d
www.leadloudacademy.com

LEADING
LADY
NETWORK

Every Queen Deserves to Be Seen

The world needs your light.
The Crown Society is a movement of women leaders who are ready to step forward, be visible, and reign with grace and strength. It's time to stop waiting in the shadows and start leading from your throne.

SCAN

JORDAN BONE:

Inspiring Positivity and Advocating for Disability Awareness

Jordan Bone is a shining example of resilience and empowerment. As a motivational speaker, author, and content creator, she has used her platform to promote positivity and raise awareness about disability. After becoming a quadriplegic at the age of 15 due to a life-changing car accident, Bone turned her personal challenges into opportunities to inspire others, advocate for accessibility, and champion self-empowerment.

Transforming Tragedy Into Purpose

In 2005, Jordan Bone's life changed forever. A devastating car accident left her paralyzed from the chest down, and she was told she would never regain the use of her hands. Facing immense physical and emotional challenges, Bone could have allowed despair to define her life. Instead, she chose a path of resilience and self-discovery, proving that adversity can lead to extraordinary strength.

"I still deserve an amazing life and so does everyone else who has a similar injury."

Bone's journey of recovery was not only about physical rehabilitation but also about redefining her sense of purpose. She found solace in creative expression, particularly through makeup, which became a medium for her to reclaim her independence and rebuild her confidence. Her passion for makeup and storytelling later evolved into a thriving social media presence, where she shares her journey with an ever-growing audience.

Spreading Positivity Through Content Creation
Jordan Bone's content resonates with millions of people worldwide. Her YouTube channel and social media platforms showcase her expertise in beauty and lifestyle while candidly addressing the realities of living with a disability. Through her videos, she demonstrates adaptive techniques for makeup application and other daily tasks, proving that creativity knows no limits.

What sets Bone apart is her authenticity and commitment to spreading positivity. She openly discusses topics like mental health, self-worth, and overcoming societal stigmas, creating a safe and inspiring space for her followers. By sharing her struggles and triumphs, Bone empowers others to embrace their uniqueness and see their challenges as opportunities for growth.

Advocacy for Accessibility and Inclusion
Beyond her role as a content creator, Jordan Bone is a passionate advocate for accessibility and inclusion. She uses her platform to raise awareness about the barriers faced by individuals with disabilities and the need for systemic change. From calling for improved accessibility in public spaces to challenging stereotypes, Bone's advocacy is rooted in the belief that everyone deserves equal opportunities to thrive.

Bone's activism extends to her collaborations with brands and organizations that prioritize inclusivity. She works tirelessly to amplify the voices of the disabled community, ensuring that their needs and experiences are recognized and respected. Her efforts have sparked important conversations about disability representation in media and beyond, paving the way for a more inclusive society.

Authoring Her Story: *My Beautiful Struggle*
In 2017, Jordan Bone released her memoir, *My Beautiful Struggle*, a heartfelt account of her journey from despair to empowerment. The book offers a raw and inspiring look at her life, detailing the emotional and physical challenges she faced after her accident and the resilience that led her to rediscover her purpose.

Through her writing, Bone shares valuable lessons about self-love, determination, and the power of positivity. Her memoir has touched the lives of readers around the world, serving as a testament to the human spirit's ability to overcome even the most daunting obstacles.

Empowering Others Through Public Speaking
As a motivational speaker, Jordan Bone captivates audiences with her powerful storytelling and uplifting message. She often speaks at schools, conferences, and corporate events, inspiring listeners to rethink their perceptions of disability and embrace a mindset of gratitude and perseverance. Her talks emphasize the importance of resilience, self-belief, and the transformative power of a positive outlook.

Bone's speeches not only inspire individuals but also challenge organizations to prioritize accessibility and inclusion. Her ability to connect with diverse audiences and foster understanding makes her a true catalyst for change.

Redefining Beauty and Strength
One of Jordan Bone's core messages is the idea that beauty and strength come in many forms. She challenges societal norms that equate beauty with perfection, encouraging people to celebrate their individuality and embrace their imperfections. By sharing her journey, she has redefined what it means to be strong, proving that vulnerability and authenticity are powerful tools for connection and growth.

Building a Legacy of Empowerment
Jordan Bone's impact reaches far beyond her online presence. As a motivational speaker, author, and advocate, she has inspired countless individuals to overcome their own obstacles and strive for a brighter future. Her unwavering commitment to promoting positivity, accessibility, and self-empowerment has made her a role model for people of all abilities.

As we honor National Speech and Hearing Awareness Month, Bone's story serves as a powerful reminder of the importance of amplifying diverse voices. Her journey from tragedy to triumph highlights the resilience of the human spirit and the transformative power of positivity. Through her work, Jordan Bone continues to break barriers, foster inclusion, and empower others to rise above their challenges and embrace their fullest potential.

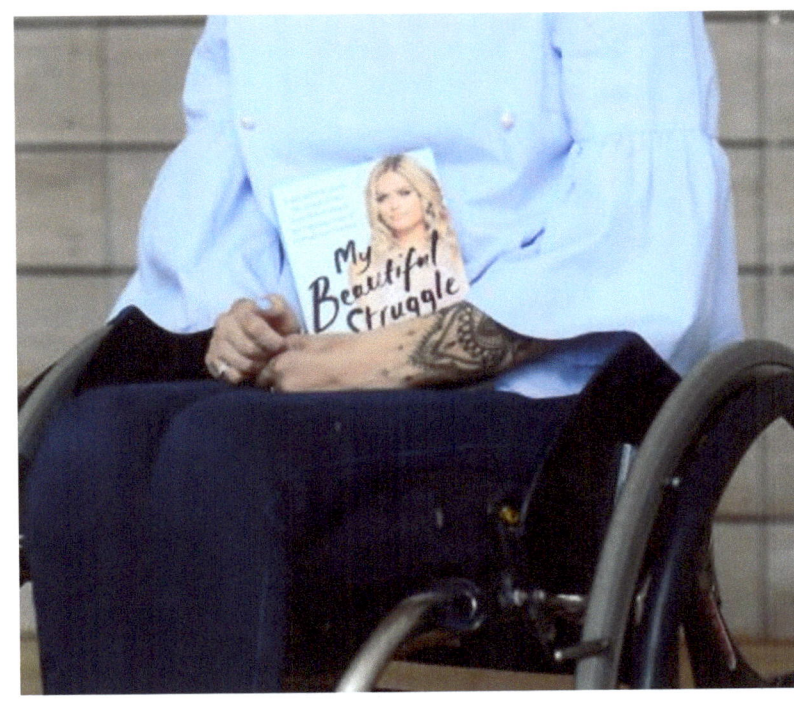

www.sherisesstudios.com

FLAWED YET FABULOUS:

How Your Unique Talents Make You Invaluable

By Michele Gunn

Your flaws are part of what makes you extraordinary. We are all uniquely created with strengths, talents, and even perceived flaws that contribute to our value. Together, we will explore how our uniqueness makes us invaluable. You will also find tips on recognizing and using your gifts effectively.

The Beauty of Imperfection
Society often pressures people to fit a mold, yet our differences are what make us special. It starts right from birth! There are expectations on how you should look, act and develop. There is no embracing your uniqueness! As we age, we are compared to other babies as well as charts on where we should be in development. Toddlers are told how to behave and that certain behaviors are *"not nice."* There is a difference between acceptable behaviors and unacceptable behaviors when it comes to safety and hurting others. Let's face it. Each one of us humans is different. We don't fit a mold. As we grow and develop into teenagers and then adults, many of us *"hide"* parts of who we are.

For example, when I was in elementary school, a teacher put tape over my mouth during class because I talked too much. I was called nosy because I enjoyed being in the know. Both of these things stifled my development and my natural talents for communication and information gathering.

Recognizing Your Unique Talents and Strengths
Everyone has God-given talents, but many people struggle to recognize them. Here are some practical ways to discover your gifts:
* Reflect on what excites you or comes naturally.
* Consider what others appreciate about you.
* Take assessments like CliftonStrengths® to gain deeper insights.
* Work with a coach to help you uncover your unique goodness.

Self-reflection and journaling are tools to track moments of success and fulfillment. You can then look for patterns to uncover your strengths. Strengths, when not used properly, can be disguised as flaws or weaknesses. A good coach can help you discern that.

Aiming Your Talents for Impact
It is important to direct your talents toward meaningful goals. Much like a musician fine-tuning their instrument, if your skills and talents aren't fine tuned, you will not achieve the desired results. Follow these tips to apply your strengths effectively:
* Align talents with a purpose or mission
* Surround yourself with people who complement your abilities.
* Continue learning and growing in your strengths.

Remember that talents are not just for personal success, but for serving and uplifting others.

Overcoming Doubt and Embracing Your Worth
We are taught from a young age to be more concerned with what is wrong with us than what is right. We are taught to second guess our decisions and to be critical of who we are, what we do and how we do it. We are ingrained with self-doubt and the fear of not being enough. It becomes part of our thinking process. Our mind begins to control us with negativity, stopping us with constant fear of failure or simply not being *"good enough."*

It's time to take control. Know your worth. Do not allow anyone (especially yourself) to diminish your value. Use your talents to serve and achieve success.

You are not flawed. You are fabulous!
When we embrace our whole selves, we step into our true calling. The world doesn't need a perfect version of you. It doesn't need more people that are molded to fit the norm. It needs the real, uniquely gifted, beautifully imperfect you. The world needs the you that you were created to be.

Connect With Michele

www.michelegunn.com
www.linkedin.com/in/michelegunn
www.facebook.com/michele.jonasgunn
www.instagram.com/michelegunn1

By Tamsyn Cornelius

ANSWERING THE CALL:

Embracing Your Creative Purpose

Creative entrepreneurship often feels less like a choice and more like a calling—an unshakable force pulling you toward self-expression. No matter how much life tries to reroute you, the desire to create always finds its way back. For me, art and creativity came as a whisper in the background of my busy life as a mom, a writer, and a freelancer. Until one day, it became impossible to ignore.

Rekindling the Creative Flame

For many years, creativity took a backseat to the demands of work and family. My days revolved around a bustling copywriting business and raising two children, while my passion for painting was reduced to small bursts of craft projects and home decor. But in 2020, when the world hit pause, I was forced to reflect. I asked myself: What gifts have I been neglecting? What do I truly have to offer the world?

So, I picked up a paintbrush again and what started as a personal challenge—to create one painting a month—quickly evolved into painting every week, then every day. Each brushstroke reignited something inside me. Soon, I found myself selling my work, creating custom commissions, and transforming a corner of my home into a dedicated art studio.

The Journey from 'Stuck' to 'Creator'

Art is more than just a pastime—it's a way of making sense of the world, a means of storytelling, and a conduit for deeper connection. Yet, many aspiring artists struggle to take that first step. If you feel creatively stuck, perhaps it is time to reignite your passion and pursue your calling. Here are some considerations...

1. Make The Time

Life is busy, but if you have a passion, you must nurture it. Block out time in your schedule to create, even if it's just an hour a week. Learn, practice, and explore different techniques. Attend workshops, take online courses, and allow yourself the space to grow.

2. Stop Comparing Yourself to Others

In a world of social media perfection, it's easy to feel inadequate. But comparison is the enemy of creativity.

Instead of measuring yourself against others, focus on improving your skills and enjoying the process. Every artist has a unique journey—embrace yours.

3. Share Your Work with the World

Fear of judgment holds many creatives back. But art is meant to be seen, felt, and experienced. Start by sharing your work with friends and family. Then, take the leap—set up an online portfolio, display your pieces at local markets, or showcase your work on social media.

4. Connect Your Creativity to a Greater Purpose

Why do you create? Understanding your deeper motivation fuels perseverance. Whether it's self-expression, storytelling, or faith-driven artistry, anchoring your work in purpose gives it meaning beyond aesthetics.

Building a Creative Life

Today, my art is more than just paintings on a canvas—it's a way to inspire, connect, and encourage others. I have since added retreat curation to my business, creating a gathering place for creativity, where I host reflective retreats and workshops, paint parties, and one-on-one mentorship sessions. I love watching people's faces light up when they create something they never thought possible.

Art has a way of awakening something dormant inside us—a forgotten passion, a buried dream, a spark of purpose. If you feel the pull toward creativity, don't ignore it. Lean in, explore, and create. The world needs what only you can bring.

Connect With Tamsyn

www.tamsyncornelius.com
www.tceditorialservices.co.za

EMBRACE GRACE & SINGLE MOTHERS

By Anna Lugo

hout out to all single mothers, single dads, and single parents. Being a single mother while pregnant was not easy. I have such admiration for Single Mothers around the world. Being a single mother was not easy but also being raised by a single widowed mother was even tougher. I watched my own mother be a single mother of 4 kids under the age of ten. Whenever i get the chance to help or assist a mother who is struggling I am the first one to say, Yes. I recently started supporting a non profit organization called "Embrace Grace".

This organization equips churches to help single and pregnant moms and their families. The goal is to take a Pro-Life stance and Pro-love action. Embrace grace exists to Inspire and equip our local churches to love on single pregnant women and young girls and their families to prepare for motherhood. These programs consists support groups for, Embrace Grace, Embrace Life, and Embrace Legacy for young mothers and fathers. Since 2012, they've helped 18,500+ mom with unexpected pregnancies to local churches in 50 states and 8 countries.

The "Embrace Grace" model is to support unexpected pregnant women in a pregnancy center, provide a love box full of supplies, a baby shower, a support group and church family to support new mothers on their new journey to motherhood. For those who feel they have nowhere to go or not one to turn to we have a solution. Their mission has always been centered around the fact that if more women knew about this great network that solely exist for them. If your interested in starting an Embrace Grace at your local church, please contact them at Embracegrace.com and become a partner of Pro-Life, Pro-Love.

I only wish I had an Embrace Grace organization to help me 45 years ago when i suddenly found myself alone at seven months pregnant. Further questions regarding this please contact me at 725-221-1511 or alohalugo@yahoo.com

Connect With Anna

www.puretealove.com
www.Women-Inspiring-women-and-men-too.com
Tiktok: @Up2uGod

she wins
Women's Network

Empowering Women Entrepreneurs to Thrive Locally and Globally

Transform your life and business with access to exclusive resources, strategic networking, and unwavering support.

Benefits:

➤ *Strategic networking & mentorship*
➤ *Masterclasses & exclusive resources*
➤ *Member spotlights & VIP perks*

Join for just

$87/MONTH

no contracts, cancel anytime.

Start thriving today. Join She Wins Women's Network!

www.shewinswomensnetwork.com

JAMEELA JAMIL:

Advocating for Mental Health and Challenging Ableism

Jameela Jamil is a force to be reckoned with. Known for her acting roles, activism, and unyielding dedication to social justice, Jamil has used her platform to challenge societal norms and champion causes like mental health, body positivity, and the fight against ableism. As the founder of the I Weigh movement, she has redefined how society measures worth, encouraging individuals to focus on their achievements and self-worth instead of conforming to unrealistic beauty standards.

From Speech Challenges to Advocacy

Jameela Jamil's journey to becoming a global advocate was shaped by her own personal experiences. Growing up in London, she struggled with speech challenges, including a stammer, which made her feel isolated and misunderstood. These challenges, however, became the foundation of her resilience and determination. Rather than letting them define her, Jamil embraced her imperfections and used them as a way to connect with others facing similar struggles.

Her openness about these experiences has been instrumental in promoting self-acceptance and breaking the stigma surrounding speech difficulties. By sharing her story, she encourages others to embrace their vulnerabilities and see them as strengths. Her advocacy highlights the importance of creating inclusive spaces where individuals can thrive without fear of judgment.

The I Weigh Movement: Redefining Worth

In 2018, Jameela Jamil launched the I Weigh movement, a social media campaign that quickly gained global attention. The movement was born out of frustration with how society often reduces individuals, particularly women, to their physical appearance. Jamil wanted to shift the narrative by encouraging people to celebrate their achievements, values, and contributions to the world.

I Weigh is more than just a hashtag; it's a community that fosters empowerment and self-love. The movement's platform amplifies diverse voices, showcasing stories of resilience and self-discovery.

By promoting mental health awareness and challenging toxic beauty standards, I Weigh has become a safe space for individuals to share their journeys and find solidarity.

Challenging Ableism and Advocating for Inclusion
Jameela Jamil's activism extends beyond mental health and body positivity to include the fight against ableism. She has been vocal about the discrimination faced by individuals with disabilities and advocates for a society that values inclusivity and accessibility. Jamil's approach is deeply intersectional, recognizing how factors like race, gender, and socioeconomic status intersect with disability to create unique challenges.

As someone who has dealt with health issues, including Ehlers-Danlos Syndrome (EDS), Jamil speaks candidly about the need for compassion and understanding toward people living with chronic conditions. Her transparency has sparked important conversations about the stigma surrounding disabilities and the importance of creating systems that support, rather than exclude, individuals with diverse needs.

Using Her Platform for Change
Jameela Jamil's rise to fame began with her acting career, particularly her breakout role as Tahani Al-Jamil on NBC's *The Good Place*. While her acting talents earned her widespread recognition, Jamil has consistently used her platform to advocate for meaningful change. Whether she's addressing the harmful impact of diet culture or calling out influential figures for perpetuating unrealistic standards, Jamil's commitment to honesty and authenticity sets her apart.

> *"Every twist and turn in life is an opportunity to learn something new about yourself, your interests, your talents, and how to set and then achieve goals. "*

Her social media presence is a testament to her dedication to activism. Jamil often engages in candid discussions about mental health, body image, and systemic discrimination, encouraging her followers to think critically about these issues. By leveraging her visibility, she has built a community of individuals who are passionate about creating a more compassionate and inclusive world.

Promoting Mental Health Awareness
A central theme of Jameela Jamil's advocacy is mental health. She has been open about her struggles with anxiety, depression, and body dysmorphia, using her experiences to shed light on the importance of seeking help and supporting others. Jamil emphasizes that mental health is just as important as physical health and calls for systemic changes to improve access to mental health resources.

Through her work with I Weigh and her public speaking engagements, Jamil normalizes conversations about mental health and encourages individuals to prioritize their well-being. She challenges the stigma that often surrounds mental illness, reminding people that seeking support is a sign of strength, not weakness.

Building a Legacy of Empowerment
Jameela Jamil's impact goes far beyond her roles on screen. As an actress, activist, and founder of I Weigh, she has dedicated her life to challenging societal norms and advocating for those who are often overlooked. Her commitment to promoting mental health, self-acceptance, and inclusion has inspired countless individuals to embrace their authentic selves.

As we celebrate National Speech and Hearing Awareness Month, Jamil's story serves as a powerful reminder of the importance of amplifying diverse voices. Her journey from facing speech challenges to becoming a global advocate highlights the transformative power of resilience, authenticity, and compassion. Through her work, Jameela Jamil continues to redefine what it means to create meaningful change, proving that when we lift each other up, we all rise.

MARRY YOURSELF:

How Chaos Can be Your Guide to Your God-Given Purpose

By Ozzin Jun

Life's most transformative lessons often emerge from the depths of personal chaos. Ozzin Jun, the author of the soon to be published book Marry Yourself in October 2025, is no stranger to adversity. A survivor of kidnapping and rape in 2019, she has turned her personal suffering into a powerful movement, helping others reclaim their self-worth, embrace their healing journey, and build an empire rooted in purpose.

Building on her mission, Ozzin Jun is a contributing author to Inspire Her which was published on 18 March 2025, a powerful book featuring stories from extraordinary women who have turned their struggles into purpose.

In her chapter, she dives deeper into how personal chaos is not a life sentence, but a tool for bigger success in life. It's a teaser of her upcoming book *"Marry Yourself"*.

The Power of Self-Marriage
In Marry Yourself, Ozzin Jun explores the concept of self-compassion, self-love, and self-worth as the foundation for healthy relationships and a fulfilling life.

The book speaks directly to those who have endured hardships, struggled with self-doubt, or felt lost in their pursuit of meaning. By using personal struggles as fuel, Ozzin encourages readers to step into their worth with faith-based foundation and create the life they were meant to live.

Her story is proof that even the darkest experiences can lead to purpose. Faith in Jesus guided her through healing, allowing her to cultivate resilience and transition from an abusive relationship to a loving one, from six-figure debt to six-figure cash months, and from chronic illness to reclaiming her health. Through the Marry Yourself process, she emphasizes surrendering to God's plan and using pain as a vehicle to step into one's calling.

From Chaos to Calling – Inspire Her Book
The Marry Yourself concept is about committing to your own growth, healing, and purpose before seeking external validation. It challenges you to embrace your deepest wounds as the raw material for transformation, using them to build a life rooted in clarity and self-worth.

Inside her chapter *"Marry Yourself: Chaos as Your Guide To Purpose"*, Ozzin shares her own experiences of overcoming deep wounds and using them as the foundation for her business, personal growth, and spiritual alignment.

One powerful tool you can apply is to rewrite your inner vows, identifying the limiting beliefs you've unconsciously accepted and replacing them with truth-driven commitments that align with God's purpose for you. Instead of waiting for someone or something to *"complete"* you, Marry Yourself encourages you to step into your full identity, knowing that fulfilment comes from Jesus, not external achievements. Even if life is good, the Marry Yourself concept will guide you to a fulfilling life through Jesus to help you reach financial, relational, and spiritual goals.

Art and Faith Meets Business Strategy

Ozzin Jun is a business artist, keynote speaker, podcaster, and strategic coach with a creative, immersive approach to success. Her work blends faith, personal transformation, and luxury with an international presence. Through writing, coaching, and speaking, she inspires thousands to embrace faith, resilience, and purpose.

Beyond her books, Ozzin has coached over 15'000 individuals in marketing, branding and sales, guiding them through personal and professional transformations. She teaches the importance of leadership, defining core values, business skills and crafting a life aligned with God's calling rather than societal expectations.

Get Your Copy Today

Inspire Her is now available. Discover stories of resilience and transformation from Ozzin and other extraordinary women. Order your copy today and step into your God-given purpose.

Connect With Ozzin

www.linktr.ee/ozzinjun

GRAB YOUR COPY NOW

WWW.AMAZON.COM/DP/1960136607

She Rises, She Leads, She Lives: Overcoming Obstacles and Thriving Against All Odds brings together Hanna Olivas and 23 remarkable women to share their powerful journeys of resilience, courage, and triumph. From personal loss to societal challenges, each story reveals the strength it takes not just to survive—but to thrive. This inspiring collection is a tribute to the unbreakable spirit of women rising against all odds.

SHE WINS

SUMMER FESTIVAL STYLING SUITE

A premier style experience uniting influencers, media, and industry insiders to celebrate fashion, beauty, health, and wellness. Discover the season's top trends and connect with leading brands.

POWERED BY SHE WINS WOMEN'S NETWORK

BECOMING UNDENIABLY U:

Reclaiming Your Identity, Voice, and Power as a Woman in Business

By Valarie Harris

What does it mean to be Undeniably U? It's not just a cute phrase—it's a movement. A mindset. A fierce return to your full, authentic self. The version of you that doesn't apologize for dreaming big, speaking loud, or standing tall in rooms that once tried to shrink you.

And who am I to tell you this?

I'm a woman who climbed the corporate ladder in retail while quietly whispering to herself, *"There's more."* I'm a military brat, a wife, a mom, a marketing strategist, and a freedom-chasing entrepreneur who was never built for a box. I've been told my way of talking wouldn't cut it, my style was *"too much,"* my passion needed to be toned down. I've heard the unspoken *"you're just a woman"* in meetings, interviews, and business deals more times than I can count.

But lucky for me, I was raised by two parents who taught me to never let the world define me. They reminded me that I wasn't here to blend in—I was here to stand out.

Undeniably U was born from that truth.

It's for every woman who's been told she's too loud, too bold, too ambitious—or not enough of something else. It's for the women like me who were never told *"no,"* just told, *"do it differently because you're a woman."* Wear this. Say that. Tone it down. Be more likable. Smile more. Don't ruffle feathers.

"You don't need to be more like them. You need to be more like you—bold, brave, and undeniably YOU."

I tried. I tried to follow the mold—until I realized I was suffocating in it.

I had to unlearn the rules written by people who didn't look like me, talk like me, or understand the fire in me. Entrepreneurship was terrifying. Releasing the steady paycheck, the structure, the *"safe path"* wasn't easy. But my spirit craved more. I had stories, skills, and a message that needed to be heard. And I wasn't about to let anyone—especially not my own self-doubt—shut that down.

Being Undeniably U means standing in your truth even when your knees are shaking.
It means building a business (and a life) that reflects your values, your voice, and your vibe.

So to the woman reading this who's scared to speak up, to launch, to pivot, to change—let me say this: You were never *"too much."* You were always meant for more.

Let this be your permission slip to:

Show up without shrinking.
Speak without second-guessing.
Dream without delay.

Because your magic doesn't live in the mold. It lives in your uniqueness. Your lived experiences. Your laughter. Your lessons. Your scars and your sparkle.

I built a brand and a business on being real, raw, and rooted in my truth. I've made mistakes. I've had wins. I've doubted myself. And still, I rise—not in spite of who I am, but because of it.

So the next time someone tells you what *"works"* in business or life, smile. Then go do it your way.

Be Unapologetic.
Be Unrelenting.
Be Undeniably U.

Connect With Valarie

www.VarrisMarketing.com
www.TimeFreedomFreak.com (Not Live Yet, but that's OK to share)
www.facebook.com/varrism
www.instagram.com/coachvalygrl1
www.linkedin.com/in/varrismarketing

THE *NEW WAVE* OF PUBLISHING:

A Path for Dreamers, Doers, and Storytellers

By Michelle Seguin

There's something sacred about holding your finished book in your hands for the first time.

It's not just paper and ink. It's proof.
Proof that you followed through.
Proof that your voice matters.
Proof that what you carried inside you for so long is finally out in the world, ready to be heard.

Yet, so many aspiring authors never get there. Not because they lack talent, but because they're afraid to begin. Or they start but get lost along the way. Life happens. Doubt creeps in. The dream gets buried beneath everyday responsibilities and the voice that whispers, Who are you to write a book?

If that's you, let me tell you something I know for sure: If you desire to write a book, somewhere inside you is the voice that can. You don't have to be perfect. You just have to begin.

That's why I created Larger Than Life Publishing: not just to help people publish books but also to help them start, stay inspired, and bring something into the world they're proud of.

I work with people who have a story inside them: memoirists, coaches, healers, helpers, and visionaries. Anyone who's lived through something and feels called to share it. Whether you're writing about your life, expertise, or a message the world needs, my role is walking beside you from the first word to the final printed page.

As a certified coach and author, I know how overwhelming it can initially feel.
That's why I make the process clear, compassionate, and deeply personal. I'm not just here to publish your book. I'm here to help you uncover its heart, draw out your most powerful message, and shape it into something that surpasses anything you thought possible.

This isn't about rigid templates or quick-fix models. It's about intention and crafting something that feels truly you, with clarity, confidence, and lasting impact.

Because let's be honest, this isn't just about the book. It's about who you become in the process.

Writing a book stretches you. It asks you to rise. It challenges the old stories you've told yourself and replaces them with a new one: the one where you showed up, spoke up, and finished what you started.

Every author I've worked with comes in with a vision and a few fears. Every one of them leaves with something more than a manuscript.

They leave with clarity, confidence, and a deep sense of ownership. They leave with a book they can hold, love, and share, and the unshakable knowledge that they created something real.

Some have told me the process helped them reconnect with parts of themselves they thought were gone. Others finally found the voice they didn't know they had. Each time, the moment they hold that first copy in their hands, it's magic. It's legacy.

That's what happens when you write with the right support.

You find your voice.
You finish what you started.
And you rise into the author you were meant to be.
You don't have to do it alone.
You don't have to know every step.
You have to say yes to the dream that's been whispering your name all along.

This is the new wave of publishing, built on truth, guided by your voice, and committed to preserving the heart of your story. It's for people who are done waiting. It's for people ready to finally write the book that's been inside them all along.

If that's you, this is your sign.

Your story is ready. And so are you.

The new wave of publishing is here and waiting for you to begin.

Connect With Michelle

www.largerthanlifepublishing.com
www.peacefulconnections.ca
www.facebook.com/largerthanlifepublishing

RECEIVE LIKE A QUEEN, GIVE LIKE A GODDESS:

The Real Secret to Unlimited Abundance

By Dawna Campbell

Let's get real. For so many of us—especially women—receiving can feel awkward as hell. Whether it's compliments, money, help, or recognition, we somehow turn it into guilt, discomfort, or a hundred reasons why we're not quite *"ready"* for it.

But what if I told you this one shift—learning how to receive with intention—could be the very thing that unlocks limitless abundance in your life?

Let me take you back to Japan.

I was shopping for a gift. Not just any gift—something special for a mentor who had deeply impacted my life. I spotted a sake set in a quirky little novelty shop. Cute. Sweet. Affordable.

But something felt off. My friend nudged me and said, *"You should check the department store."*

I'll be honest, I didn't want to. Time was tight. But I went. And there, tucked into a glowing display of elegant ceramics, was a collection of the most stunning sake sets I'd ever seen. Like, jaw-dropping gorgeous. The kind of beauty that made you stop breathing for a second.

And then I looked at the price tag.
Cue panic.

"This is too much," I told myself. *"This is luxury. It's just a gift."*

But my friend looked at me and dropped the wisdom bomb that changed everything:
"It's about where you choose to receive from. If you go where the value is, that means you are open to receiving that value. You have the privilege to receive."

Boom.
It hit me like a cosmic slap across the face.

That was the moment I got it.
Receiving isn't selfish. Receiving isn't shameful. Receiving isn't excess.
Receiving is preparation for sharing. It's how you multiply the blessing.

See, most of us were taught that generosity is about sacrifice. That to give, you must go without. But what if that belief is what's actually blocking abundance.

What if the flow of abundance depends on how well you receive it—and how freely you let it move through you? Let me drop some real talk on you. *"Abundance is not something we hold—it's something we host."* Wealth, love, wisdom, opportunity... they don't belong to us. They move through us.

When you receive with openness and give with generosity, you become a channel instead of a container. And that's where the magic happens.

You ever try to hold water in your hands for too long? It slips through your fingers, right?

When you let it flow—through pipes, rivers, channels—it moves, it spreads, it multiplies. That's what abundance does. It grows when you circulate it. Not when you hoard it. Not when you cling to it in fear. Not when you think, *"If I give this away, there won't be enough left for me."*

That is scarcity talking. That is fear pretending to be wisdom.

So here's the shift:
Next time you receive—whether it's money, support, joy, praise, or divine inspiration—don't stop the flow.

Ask yourself:
How can I let this move through me?
Who else can benefit from what I just received?
How do I turn this moment into a ripple effect?

Because the more you give, the more space you create to receive. The more you receive, the more power you have to give. It's a feedback loop of expansion. And it works every damn time.

So whether it's a luxurious sake set or a sacred piece of wisdom... receive it fully. Not just for you—but for what it will become through you.

Abundance is not meant to stop with you.
It's meant to start with you.

Connect With Dawna

www.bookdawna.com
www.bettercalldawna.com
www.linkedin.com/in/dawnacampbell
www.instagram.com/dawnacampbellofficial
www.facebook.com/dawna.campbell.71

FENIX TV

SHE RISES STUDIOS

she wins

NICE GIRLS FINISH FIRST

SHE WINS
VIRTUAL SUMMIT 2025

When: May 14–16, 2025
Where: Exclusively on FENIX TV
Tickets: $49.97

Join us for the **She Wins Virtual Summit 2025**, a 3-day event celebrating women entrepreneurs and leaders from around the world. This year's theme, **"Nice Girls Finish First,"** showcases how kindness, empathy, and integrity drive success in business and life.

What to Expect:

- Inspiring stories from women leaders.
- Expert advice on leadership, resilience, and growth.
- Strategies for thriving in business without compromising values.

BE PART OF THIS EMPOWERING MOVEMENT AND DISCOVER HOW KINDNESS LEADS TO GREATNESS!

THE *GRIEF* NO ONE TALKS ABOUT:
3 Steps to Healing

By Danica Alison

What do you do with grief that has no funeral, no condolences, no clear goodbye? The kind that lingers in the spaces where someone should be but isn't. The loss of a child you loved but weren't meant to keep. The unraveling of a relationship that faded without closure. The moment you wake up and realize you no longer recognize yourself.

Some losses are obvious. The world acknowledges them and offers support. Others slip through the cracks, leaving you wondering, Does this even count? Am I allowed to grieve this?

I know this grief. I felt it when I lost my marriage, not just the relationship but the version of myself inside it. I felt it when I said goodbye to foster children, knowing they were never mine to keep but loving them as if they were. I felt it when I realized my identity was shifting, unsure of who I was beyond the roles I had always filled.

There is no roadmap for these kinds of losses, but I've learned that there are three steps that can help with healing.

1. Name Your Grief. It's Real

One of the hardest things about ambiguous and disenfranchised grief is that it often goes unrecognized. Without a death certificate or a formal goodbye, it's easy to feel like your pain isn't valid. But grief is not just about death. it's about loss.

Maybe you lost a relationship, but there was no breakup, just distance. Maybe you're mourning a parent who is still alive but emotionally unavailable. Maybe you miss the person you used to be before trauma reshaped you.

Naming your loss gives it weight. It allows you to say, *"This happened. This matters. I am allowed to grieve at this."*

2. Let Go of the Need for Closure

We often hear that *"closure"* is the goal of healing. But when loss is ongoing or unresolved, waiting for closure can keep us stuck.

Ambiguous grief lingers because there's no finality. You may still love someone who is no longer in your life.

You may still feel the pull of an identity that no longer fits. Instead of seeking closure, try to find ways to hold both grief and growth at the same time.

Healing does not mean erasing what was lost. It means learning how to carry it differently.

3. Find Validation. Even If Others Don't Give It

Disenfranchised grief can be isolating because the world often doesn't acknowledge it. Maybe people tell you, It wasn't really your child. You'll find someone else. You should be over it by now. Their words might make you question your own emotions.

But you don't need permission to grieve. The loss of a foster child, a divorce, a friendship that faded, the person you used to be before life changed you—all of it is real. And you deserve support, even if others don't understand.

If no one around you validates your grief, validate yourself. Find spaces where you can process it safely. Talk to those who do understand. Give yourself permission to feel, without apologizing for it.

Healing is Possible

Grief without closure or recognition can feel impossible to navigate. Grief doesn't just go away. It shifts, reshapes, and becomes part of your story. But it doesn't have to define you. Healing isn't about forgetting. It's about learning to carry it in a way that allows you to move forward.

And you don't have to do it alone.

If you're carrying grief that feels invisible, I see you. If you're navigating loss that doesn't fit inside the usual expectations, you are not alone.

Connect With Danica

www.DanicaAlison.com
www.Linktr.ee/DanicaAlison

CHAMPIONING ACCESSIBILITY:

The Inspiring Story of *Haben Girma*

Haben Girma has become a beacon of hope and empowerment for individuals with disabilities. As the first deafblind graduate of Harvard Law School, Girma has defied societal expectations and broken barriers to advocate for accessibility and inclusion. Through her work as a disability rights advocate, author, and public speaker, she has transformed challenges into opportunities to create a more equitable world.

Overcoming Barriers and Embracing Identity

Haben Girma was born in California to Eritrean and Ethiopian parents who sought refuge in the United States. She was born with limited vision and hearing due to a rare condition called Usher syndrome. Growing up, she often faced environments that lacked accessibility, yet her family's unwavering support and her determination allowed her to embrace her identity and excel academically.

Girma's journey to becoming a disability rights advocate began with her firsthand experiences of exclusion. From inaccessible textbooks to physical spaces that weren't designed with disabilities in mind, she recognized the systemic barriers faced by millions worldwide. Instead of letting these obstacles define her, Girma developed a vision for a more inclusive society where accessibility is a fundamental right, not an afterthought.

Trailblazing at Harvard Law School

Haben Girma's achievements reached new heights when she became the first deafblind student to graduate from Harvard Law School in 2013. Her time at Harvard was not without challenges; she relied on innovative technology, such as a digital Braille device, to communicate and navigate her studies. Despite these hurdles, she excelled, demonstrating that disability is not a limitation but a source of strength.

Her success at Harvard opened doors for her to advocate for individuals with disabilities on a global scale. Girma often emphasizes that accessibility benefits everyone. Whether it's designing a building with ramps or creating websites with screen reader compatibility, inclusive solutions improve experiences for all users, not just those with disabilities.

Advocacy and Public Speaking

Girma's advocacy work has taken her to stages around the world, where she speaks passionately about the importance of inclusion. She collaborates with businesses, educational institutions, and government agencies to promote policies that prioritize accessibility. Her public speaking engagements are known for their engaging, thought-provoking nature, as she shares personal anecdotes and actionable insights to inspire change.

In 2019, Girma published her memoir, *Haben: The Deafblind Woman Who Conquered Harvard Law*. The book offers a candid and inspiring account of her life, detailing her experiences as a deafblind woman navigating a world that often overlooks people with disabilities. Through her storytelling, she invites readers to challenge their own biases and think critically about how society can do better.

Promoting Innovation for Inclusion

A key aspect of Haben Girma's advocacy is her focus on innovation. She encourages technology developers to prioritize accessibility from the start, ensuring that products and services are inclusive for users of all abilities. For example, Girma has worked with companies to improve accessible technology, from apps to hardware, making it easier for individuals with disabilities to participate fully in everyday life.

Her work has earned her recognition from numerous organizations and institutions.

"Disability is not something an individual overcomes. I'm still disabled. I'm still Deafblind. People with disabilities are successful when we develop alternative techniques and our communities choose inclusion."

Girma has been honored with awards such as the White House Champions of Change and Forbes 30 Under 30. These accolades underscore the impact of her efforts and the importance of her message.

Breaking Down Stigmas

In addition to promoting accessibility, Girma is committed to breaking down stigmas surrounding disabilities. She often challenges misconceptions, emphasizing that people with disabilities are capable, talented, and deserving of equal opportunities. By sharing her story and advocating for systemic change, she has inspired countless individuals to recognize the value of diversity and inclusion.

Girma also highlights the intersectionality of her experiences as a deafblind woman of African descent. Her advocacy extends beyond disability rights to encompass issues of racial and gender equity, demonstrating the interconnectedness of social justice movements.

Building a Legacy of Inclusion

Haben Girma's work has created a ripple effect, inspiring individuals and organizations to rethink how they approach accessibility. Her vision for an inclusive society—where technology, education, and public spaces are designed to accommodate everyone—has become a guiding light for change.

As we celebrate National Speech and Hearing Awareness Month, Girma's story reminds us of the transformative power of resilience, innovation, and advocacy. Her legacy is not just one of breaking barriers but of building bridges, fostering a world where everyone has the opportunity to thrive. Through her unwavering commitment to accessibility and inclusion, Haben Girma continues to lead by example, proving that when we create space for all voices, we build a brighter future for everyone.

The Two *Most Popular Fat Loss* Eating *Strategies*

By Teri Katzenberger

- Intermittent Fasting (IF)
- Six Small Meals a Day

Both have their loyal fans. But which one is more effective? And more importantly, which one fits your lifestyle and goals?

Let's take a closer look:
- **Intermittent Fasting.** Intermittent fasting is all about when you eat—not necessarily what you eat. This strategy involves cycling between periods of eating and fasting.

Some popular IF schedules include:
- **16:8 Method** – Fast for 16 hours, eat during an 8-hour window
- **5:2 Method** – Eat normally five days a week, restrict calories for two

Pros:
- Can help with appetite control
- May improve insulin sensitivity
- Often leads to reduced calorie intake naturally

Things to consider:
- May not work well if you prefer to eat breakfast
- Energy dips or hunger pangs may happen early on
- Can take time to adjust

How to Eat for the Best Results
When it comes to fat loss, food matters—a lot. But it's not just what you eat that counts. How much and how often you eat also play a huge role in your results.

That's why the question of how to eat for optimal fat loss is one I hear all the time from clients. So let's break down two of the most talked-about strategies and figure out which one might be the right fit for YOU.

Intermittent Fasting
Intermittent fasting is an eating strategy that cycles between periods of eating and periods of fasting.

The focus isn't necessarily on what you eat, but when you eat.

There are several popular methods
- **16:8 method** – Fast for 16 hours, eat within an 8-hour window (ex: 12 PM to 8 PM).
- **5:2 method** – Eat normally for five days, then restrict calories to around 500–600 for two non-consecutive days.
- **Eat-Stop-Eat** – A full 24-hour fast once or twice per week.

Many people find that intermittent fasting helps with appetite control, better digestion, and even mental clarity. It can also naturally reduce your calorie intake without counting every bite.

Some people feel great skipping breakfast, while others feel sluggish or irritable. The key is listening to your body and finding a rhythm that works with your lifestyle.

Six Small Meals
On the flip side, the six-small-meals-a-day strategy encourages you to eat every 2–3 hours to keep your metabolism humming and hunger at bay.

Each meal is smaller and typically balanced with protein, healthy fats, and complex carbs.

This approach can:
- Help stabilize blood sugar levels
- Prevent overeating at mealtimes
- Support steady energy throughout the day

People who thrive on routine and love structure often do well with this method. However, for some, it can feel like you're constantly planning or eating—so it must be something you can realistically maintain.

So...Which One is Right for You?

What to consider:
- **Your lifestyle:** Are you constantly on the go, or do you have time to prep and plan meals?
- **Your body's signals:** Do you feel energized by fasting or do you need fuel more frequently?
- **Your goals:** Is your focus fat loss, muscle gain, energy, or just feeling better day to day?

Ultimately, both strategies can work—if you stay consistent, eat quality food, and avoid overeating (under-eating) during your eating windows.

Bottom Line
There's no one-size-fits-all when it comes to eating for fat loss. The best results come when you choose a method that fits your life, supports your goals, and makes you feel GOOD—physically and mentally.

Need help figuring out what works best for you? Let's chat—I've helped dozens of clients find their sweet spot, and I'd love to help you too.

Connect With Teri

www.livewellnow.academy
www.livewellnowacademy.com
www.facebook.com/TeriKatzenberger
www.instagram.com/TeriKatzenberger

SHE RISES
S T U D I O S

JOIN THE SRS COMMUNITY

WHERE WOMEN RISE TOGETHER!

Connect. Empower. Thrive. Whether you're an entrepreneur, professional, or simply seeking inspiration, **this is your space to grow!**

- Daily Motivation
- Expert Insights
- Sisterhood & Support

You don't have to do it alone—let's rise together!

JOIN NOW!

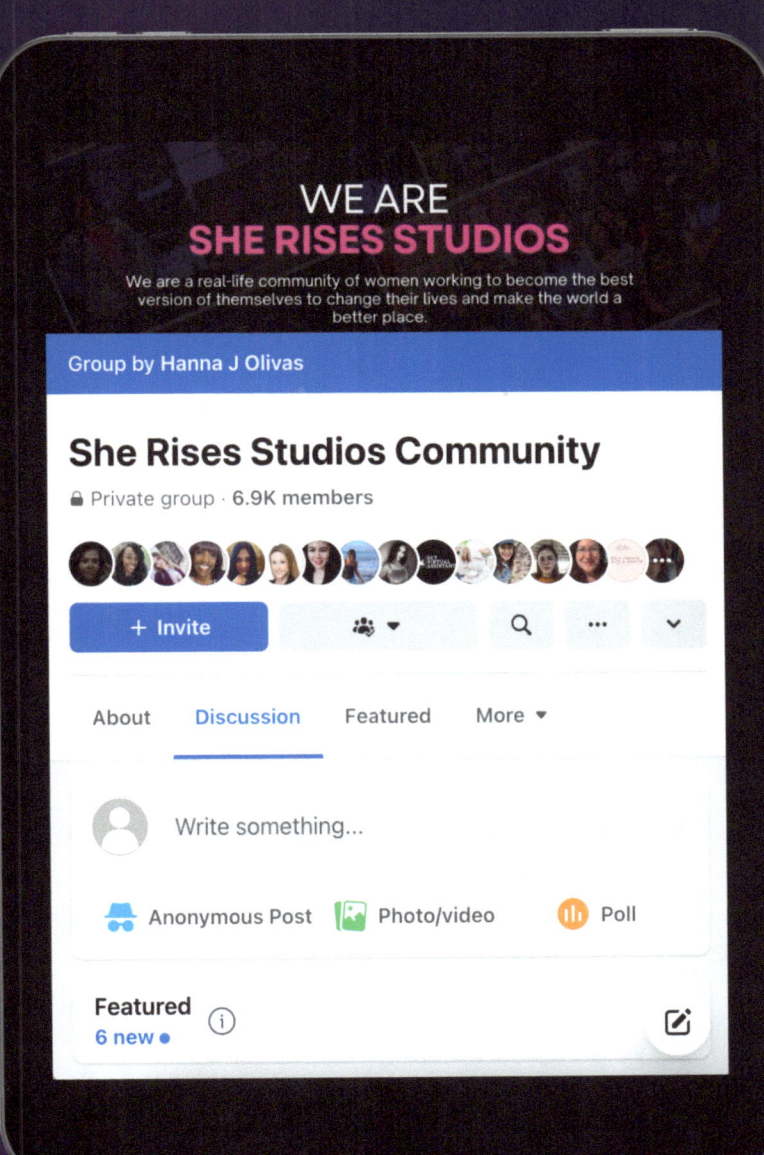

WE ARE
SHE RISES STUDIOS

We are a real-life community of women working to become the best version of themselves to change their lives and make the world a better place.

Group by Hanna J Olivas

She Rises Studios Community
🔒 Private group · 6.9K members

+ Invite

About   **Discussion**   Featured   More ▾

Write something...

🕵 Anonymous Post   🖼 Photo/video   📊 Poll

Featured ⓘ
6 new ●

www.bit.ly/srscommunitygroup   www.sherisesstudios.com

MEET *ELISE MORGAN:*

*The Powerhouse Behind The Elise Morgan
Experience Podcast*

Elise Morgan is a former personal trainer, fitness model, professional athlete turned life coach, author, speaker, and healer on a mission to help you reclaim your power and create a life you love. Known for her bold, no-nonsense attitude and infectious energy, Elise brings personal development to life with a twist of sass, humor, and authenticity. Her podcast, The Elise Morgan Experience, is a journey of transformation where no topic is off the table, and every conversation leaves you empowered and ready to take action.

Elise's path to becoming the force she is today wasn't without its struggles. From overcoming toxic relationships and people-pleasing habits to navigating life's toughest challenges, Elise's story is one of resilience and self-discovery. Her own experiences have shaped her approach to coaching and personal development—showing that anyone, no matter what , can unlock their potential and live a life they love.

THE ELISE MORGAN EXPERIENCE

Elise dives into the real, raw aspects of life with a unique perspective. This podcast is for anyone looking to level up and break free from living a limited life. Whether you're dealing with divorce, grief, PTSD, the loss of loved ones, betrayal, or simply want advice and guidance on having confidence and showing up as the best version of yourself, Elise's podcast is a space to find inspiration, actionable advice, and powerful stories. She talks a lot about the law of attraction, manifesting, and mindset, all of which can help you create the life you deserve.

But Elise isn't alone in this journey. Some of her episodes features exciting guests who bring expertise from a wide range of areas, from personal development and dating to overcoming trauma and finding inner peace. It's a podcast that caters to but not limited to women ,for those ready to make a change and take control of their lives. Elise believes that the key to transformation is a shift in mindset, and she and her guests provide the insights and tools you need to make that shift.

"I believe in the power of the mind ," Elise says. *"Life doesn't have to keep you stuck. We all have the ability to design a life that aligns with who we really are, and that's what this podcast is all about—helping you wake up to the power within you!"*

With each episode, Elise challenges her listeners to take responsibility , bold action and stop waiting for permission to live the life they deserve. Whether it's learning how to set boundaries, heal from past wounds, or cultivate a positive mindset, Elise provides practical advice that's grounded in real-life experiences.

Elise's podcast is a blend of personal development, spirituality, and real talk. It's not just about listening; it's about implementing what you learn into your life , the shifts that will transform how you show up in the world. By weaving her expertise as a life coach with her candid, no-nonsense attitude, Elise helps you navigate the ups and downs of life with clarity, confidence, and grace.

As Elise continues to build her brand, she's creating a space for people to connect, learn, and grow. From one-on-one coaching to workshops and retreats, Elise's goal is to help people tap into their power and create their version of happiness, success, and fulfillment. It's all part of The Elise Morgan Experience, a movement as Elise describes *"to help you live a life you F-In love"*

So, if you're ready to transform your life, break free from self-doubt, and create the future you've always dreamed of, The Elise Morgan Experience is the podcast for you.

Connect With Elise

www.instagram.com/theelisemorganexperience
www.youtube.com/@TheEliseMorganExperience
www.podcasts.apple.com/us/podcast/the-elise-morgan-experience-real-talk-on-real-life/id1719459894
elisemorgan@coachelisemorgan.com

Your Story *Matters!*

By Dani Rosenblad James

When it comes to being open about a personal story, many people may stop before the words leave their pen. They don't even allow it to touch paper because of their inner blocks. That feeling of self-doubt starts to swirl in your stomach and it makes you sick. I completely understand that! As I worked on my personal story, that same thing happened to me a couple of times. But you know what?! I didn't let that stop me!

I used it as fuel to drive me to finish it and press that button to send it off to She Rises Studios to be published. I knew that my story could help others since I had talked over and over again about my story on podcasts prior to starting my writing journey. Now, some might say that, *"Well, yeah that worked for you. But my story isn't worth it."*

Believe in your Story!
That's crap! I truly believe every story matters! There are so many people on this planet living their lives. It's hard to believe that NO ONE would connect with your story. You could be the voice for the ones that are voiceless about a topic or experience similar to what they went through. You could be the one that's brave to hold up your story when it's about your personal family strife. So, all you need to do to make this happen is GET OUT OF YOUR OWN WAY!

I know this is easier said than done. I get it. I'm relearning this as I'm working on my second book. But you know what? Even though this book is more personal and is dragging my family into it, I have this feeling that it NEEDS to get out there! There are people out there that have been dealing with something similar that's in my story and I know this book would mean a lot to them.

So, why should I hold out to them? Because of fear, or of being judged? I could let that stop me, but I see more benefits of getting it out than not.

I Served my Heart on a Platter
When I published my first book, I had felt as though I was serving my heart on a platter for all to see. It hurts to think about it as an open wound for all. But I got out of my own way and I did that by journaling and getting to the bottom of my problem. I finally discovered that I was scared, I was shaking with fear to get such a personal book out there to the public that I almost didn't do it.

Now, I don't want anyone to put their heart out there only to get cold feet right before publishing. This is why I have created a free writing community where I can help you on the whole writing process. Then, I suggest She Rises Studios among a few other publishing companies that you can choose from. That decision is all up to you. But as you're writing, it's nice to see that you're not alone! There's a community with help along the way!

Stop Finding Excuses and Start Writing!
So, that kid version of you probably has been waiting for you to write a book for a long time. When is the time it's going to happen? Many people tend to postpone it over and over. That's a great way to make it NOT happen. If you truly want to write a book, stop procrastinating and start the process. It's worth getting it out there and you can just do this for you! When you're able to say that you're an author, it feels nice and rewarding! It's time! Start writing your book now!

Connect With Dani

www.misfitwanders.com
www.linkedin.com/in/dani-rosenblad-james-709231179
www.instagram.com/misfit_wanders
www.facebook.com/danielle.james.3958

REBECCA ALEXANDER:

Resilience and Advocacy for the Deafblind Community

Rebecca Alexander is a powerful voice for the deafblind community, a bestselling author, psychotherapist, and disability advocate whose life story is a testament to resilience and determination. Living with Usher syndrome—a genetic condition that causes progressive loss of both hearing and vision—Alexander has transformed her personal challenges into a mission to inspire others and raise awareness for individuals with disabilities.

Navigating Life with Usher Syndrome
Diagnosed with Usher syndrome in her teens, Rebecca Alexander faced the reality of gradually losing her sight and hearing. Despite the daunting prognosis, she refused to let her condition define her or limit her aspirations. Instead, Alexander adopted a mindset of adaptability and perseverance, channeling her energy into building a fulfilling life and career.

Her journey has been marked by both physical and emotional challenges, but Alexander's ability to maintain a positive outlook has set her apart. By embracing the unknown and finding creative ways to navigate her evolving senses, she has become a role model for others facing similar obstacles.

Sharing Her Story Through Writing
In her memoir, Not Fade Away: A Memoir of Senses Lost and Found, Rebecca Alexander provides a deeply personal account of her life with Usher syndrome. The book chronicles her experiences of growing up with the condition, adapting to its challenges, and finding meaning and joy in life despite the difficulties.

Not Fade Away is more than just a memoir; it's a celebration of the human spirit. Alexander's writing is candid and heartfelt, offering readers a window into her world while inspiring them to overcome their own struggles. The memoir has resonated with audiences worldwide, earning critical acclaim for its authenticity and impact.

Advocating for the Deafblind Community
As a disability advocate, Rebecca Alexander is passionate about promoting awareness and understanding of the deafblind community. She uses her platform to shed light on the unique challenges faced by individuals living with dual sensory loss and to advocate for greater accessibility and inclusion.

Alexander has worked tirelessly to amplify the voices of the deafblind community, collaborating with organizations and participating in public speaking engagements to educate others. Her advocacy emphasizes the importance of breaking down barriers and creating opportunities for people with disabilities to thrive in all aspects of life.

A Career in Helping Others
Rebecca Alexander's commitment to helping others extends to her work as a psychotherapist. With a Master's degree in Social Work and Public Health, she provides counseling and support to individuals navigating their own mental health challenges. Her unique perspective as someone living with Usher syndrome allows her to connect deeply with her clients and offer insights rooted in empathy and lived experience.

Through her practice, Alexander empowers others to embrace their strengths, confront their fears, and cultivate resilience. Her work underscores the importance of mental health and the role it plays in overall well-being, particularly for individuals facing life-altering circumstances.

Inspiring Resilience Through Public Speaking
Rebecca Alexander's ability to inspire others goes beyond her writing and therapeutic work. As a sought-after public speaker, she delivers motivational talks that resonate with audiences of all backgrounds. Her speeches focus on themes of resilience, adaptability, and finding joy amidst adversity, leaving listeners feeling uplifted and empowered.

Alexander often speaks at conferences, schools, and corporate events, sharing her story and advocating for a more inclusive society. Her authenticity and relatability make her a compelling speaker, and her message of hope and determination has a lasting impact on those who hear her.

Promoting Awareness and Inclusion
One of Alexander's key missions is to promote awareness and inclusion for individuals with disabilities. She advocates for accessible technology, improved healthcare, and greater representation of the deafblind community in media and public life.

"Breathe in peace, breathe out fear."

Her efforts aim to challenge misconceptions and highlight the diverse experiences and contributions of people with disabilities.

By sharing her own journey, Alexander inspires others to view disability through a lens of strength and possibility rather than limitation. Her advocacy encourages society to create spaces where everyone can thrive, regardless of their abilities.

Living Life Fully
Rebecca Alexander's life is a testament to the power of resilience and the importance of living fully, even in the face of adversity. Whether she's hiking mountains, cycling, or practicing yoga, Alexander embraces each day with gratitude and determination. Her ability to find joy and purpose in life serves as an inspiration to others, reminding them that challenges can be opportunities for growth.

As we honor National Speech and Hearing Awareness Month, Rebecca Alexander's story highlights the importance of amplifying diverse voices and fostering inclusion. Her journey of resilience, advocacy, and self-discovery reminds us of the value of compassion and the impact of breaking down barriers for a more inclusive world.

Explore Insights and Embrace *Transformation*

TUNE IN NOW &
LISTEN TO THE PODCAST

Beyond to Freedom

WITH **PAULA C LAMB**

CHAOS, CRAYONS, AND CARDIOLOGY:

Why Medical Moms Need More Than Coffee to Survive

By K. Crystal Griffith, Founder of Medical Mom Warriors™

There's a very specific type of silence that descends in the ER at 2 a.m. when the triage nurse squints at your child's chart, furrows her brow, and then whispers, *"Hang tight, the doctor will be right in."* You know the one. That's not just a warning bell —it's the unofficial national anthem of Medical Mom Land.

I didn't get a welcome packet when I arrived here. No guidebook. No matching T-shirts. Just a complex diagnosis, a free pen from a neurologist, and an invitation to a life that no one dreams about... but many of us are now living in vivid, unfiltered color.

This isn't just parenting. This is combat caregiving.

It's waking up to alarms—IV pumps, oxygen monitors, insurance hold music—and still finding the strength to make gluten-free mickey-shaped pancakes.

It's pretending you're calm during another ambulance ride while your insides are screaming, *"God, help! Not again."*

It's knowing your child's anatomy better than some med students and fiercely advocating at IEP meetings like a cross between a lawyer, a lioness, and a lunch-deprived caffeine junkie.

And yet... it's lonely here.

The average mom group doesn't cover the topics we deal with. *"How to sneak vegetables into dinner"* doesn't quite cut it when your kid's nutrition is delivered via a G-tube and you're trying to figure out how to sanitize syringes without looking like a meth chemist on the go.

That's why I created Medical Mom Warriors™— because the sisterhood we need doesn't exist in typical spaces.

Our community was born out of late nights, tear-streaked prayers, unanswered voicemails, and that burning question every one of us has whispered into the void: *"Am I the only one doing this?"*

No, sweet warrior. You're not.

We are a battalion of moms who fight not only for our children's lives but also for our own sanity, identity, and spiritual survival. We do the research, learn the acronyms, track the symptoms, and hold the line—even when our knees are shaking and our faith is clinging on by a thread.

And here's the kicker: we laugh too.

Laughter is holy medicine in our world. Like the time I labeled my daughter's EpiPen case *"Jesus, take the injector"* because humor and hope have to coexist if we're going to make it.

That's the heartbeat of Medical Mom Warriors™—we offer resources, real talk, and ridiculous encouragement for the days you're one more denial letter away from turning into a feral raccoon in the hospital parking lot.

We walk with you through the hard stuff:
- How to manage appointments without losing your mind
- How to advocate without losing your voice
- How to care for your child without losing yourself

And we don't just survive—we build each other back up with Scripture, strategy, and sass.

The biggest pain point we see? Isolation.
So we built a sisterhood.
The second biggest? Feeling under-equipped.
So we built toolkits, training, and tangible transformation.

Because you weren't meant to walk this alone.

So whether you're new to this world or you've already earned your honorary MD in *"All the Things Nobody Warned Me About,"* you are welcome here. We see you. We believe in you. We saved you a seat. (Probably next to someone who has a laminator fetish for medical binders.)

It's time to pick up your sword.

You are not just surviving—
You are a Medical Mom Warrior.

Come join us.

Connect With K. Crystal

Medical Mom Warriors

www.MedicalMomWarriors.com

STILL *RISING:*

A Mother's Day Story of Resilience, Purpose & Power

By Jo Ann Nider

As I reflect on Mother's Day and the women in my life, I am reminded not just of the legendary women who came before us, but of the quiet warriors, the everyday heroes, and the modern-day trailblazers who rise in the face of adversity. I am one of them.

I am a wife of 32 years, a proud mother of three incredible adult children, a businesswoman, mentor and a Warrior of Multiple Myeloma, along with several autoimmune diseases. My journey is not one I would have chosen, but it has shaped me in the most powerful way. Each chapter brought lessons, but it was during the most difficult time that I found my strength.

Living with an incurable cancer and my various medical issues has not slowed me down. It has made my purpose clearer: to help women rise, organize their lives from the inside out, and thrive. Whether through my organizing business, Jo Ann's Creations or through leadership and community, I continue to show up for women, because I know what it means to need someone to believe in you. We must also encourage and instill that same belief, bravery, hope, and perseverance in our daughters. They are watching, and the baton is not just passed but placed in their hands with purpose.

Legacy of Strength: A Mother's Day Reflection
One of the greatest gifts of my life has been the incredible opportunity to know and love my mother-in-law, Olga—a 99-year-old Holocaust survivor whose legacy continues to shape our family.

At just 15 years old, in 1941, Olga's life changed forever when Hungary joined the war. By 1944, she and her sister Clara had endured slave labor battalions, Ravensbrück Concentration Camp, and a brutal Death March. Clara was ready to give up, but Olga insisted they keep going. *"Mother would never forgive me if I came home without you,"* she said.

After the war ended, Olga's family ultimately migrated to Uruguay. Samuel, who she met after the war, followed Olga to Uruguay where they married. Olga opened a hair salon, had a son (my husband Dan) and later immigrated to New York so they could reunite with Samuel's only surviving sibling.

Years later, Olga began sharing her story; first through Steven Spielberg's Shoah Foundation, where her story is preserved in the U.S. Holocaust Memorial Museum in Washington, D.C. She then began to tell her story to students during their studies of the Holocaust throughout New Jersey.

But I cannot talk about rising without also reflecting on my own mother Ella, who taught me what motherhood truly means. My mom raised five children while my father worked in NYC road construction, and she did it with strength and an incredible work ethic. She married at 18 and raised four daughters and one son.

As the town's local seamstress, my mom was always busy altering and making clothes. She made beautiful wedding gowns including my own. She didn't stop there; when she wasn't sewing for others, she made a lot of our clothes, dresses, bathing suits, Halloween costumes etc. My mom also made beautiful doll dresses, accessories, and seasonal decor for our home, including curtains and decorations. As we grew older, my mom continued to sew. This is when my creativity came out. We collaborated on everything she made for me. She made skirts, blouses, dresses and even a suit.

But my mom's gifts weren't just in her hands; they were in her heart. She taught me how to cook as my grandmother taught her. We had home-cooked meals every night of the week, a cherished tradition I carried on with my family.

My mom passed away a year and a half ago after a long battle with dementia. I will, however, forever carry her lessons with me, not just as a mother but as a woman. She lived for her husband and her children. She raised us to be strong, creative, and kind; traits I hope to pass on to my own children.

In part, because they survived... I thrive. Because they rose... I rise. And because the women in my life, past and present, never gave up, I will never stop fighting for my life.

On this Mother's Day, as we honor the women who have shaped our lives, our mother's grandmother, sisters, friends, and mentors who continue to walk beside us we remember that their strength is our legacy. A legacy to be passed on to those who come after us, like my daughters Rachel and Jessica, watching, learning and preparing to lead *"It's Time to Live."*

Connect With Jo Ann

Joanider@gmail.com
www.instagram.com/livelifefullywithcancer
www.facebook.com/jo.a.nider
www.shewinswomensnetwork.com/?ref=10

UNSHAKEABLE:

The Story of a Woman Who Chose to Rise

By Monica Connolly

For many women, life becomes a balancing act of caregiving, career, and responsibilities, often at the expense of their own well-being and dreams. I know this struggle because I lived it.

For years, I was the one everyone relied on—the caregiver, the provider, the one holding everything together. I believed strength meant sacrificing my needs, pushing through exhaustion, and making sure everyone else was okay. It nearly cost me my life.

I'll never forget sitting in a doctor's office, exhausted and in pain, hearing the words that shook me to my core:
"If you don't make drastic changes, you are going to die soon."

At the time, I was battling severe obesity, chronic pain, and a heart condition. But what most people didn't know was that I was also struggling with a binge eating disorder. Food had become my comfort, my escape, and the way I coped with emotions I didn't know how to process.

I didn't even recognize the woman looking back at me. I wasn't just physically sick—I was emotionally and spiritually depleted. I had spent years pouring into everyone else, and there was nothing left for me.

That was my breaking point—but also my turning point.
I made a choice: I wasn't just going to survive—I was going to heal and thrive.

Over the next two years, I lost 150 pounds, but more importantly, I gained myself back. I healed my gut, rewired my mindset, and redefined who I was—not just for me, but for the women I knew were suffering in silence.

Through that transformation, I discovered a powerful truth: women are constantly told to put themselves last. They push through and try to be everything for everyone, and in the process, they lose themselves.

I knew I had to help change that narrative. That's why I became a Certified Holistic Health Coach, Master Life Coach, and Mindset Transformation Expert. My coaching isn't just about weight loss or wellness—it's about helping women reclaim their identity, reset their health, and realign with their purpose.

True transformation happens when we build lives that reflect our values and passions. For many women, that means stepping into entrepreneurship—not just to earn income, but to create businesses that leave a lasting legacy.

Through my Rise & Thrive coaching programs, I help women gain clarity, rebuild confidence, and take empowered action in their health, mindset, and leadership. Whether they're just starting their wellness journey or ready to launch a book, podcast, or business, I provide the accountability, tools, and strategy they need to grow.

That's why I also created:

- **Ember to Empire: A Women's Collective** – A networking and leadership community for ambitious women ready to rise.
- **The Rise & Thrive Mastermind** – A space for launching purpose-driven businesses and stepping into bold visibility.
- **The Unshakeable Belief Podcast** – Where I share real stories and strategies to help women build belief and take action.
- **My Upcoming Book, Made for More** – A guide to help women break free from limitations and embrace transformation.

If there's one thing I want every woman reading this to know, it's this:
You are not stuck. You are not broken. You are ready for more.

I know what it feels like to be exhausted and uncertain. But when a woman decides to take back her power, everything changes.

My mission is to educate, mentor, and empower the next generation of women leaders and changemakers. Because when women rise, families thrive, communities grow, and we build a ripple effect of impact that lasts for generations.

Now let's rise.

Connect With Monica

www.monicaconnollycoaching.com
www.facebook.com/monica.a.connolly.7
www.linkedin.com/in/mnconnolly
www.instagram.com/monicaconnollyandco

GRAB YOUR COPY NOW

WWW.AMAZON.COM/DP/1960136666

In She Grows Stronger, Hanna Olivas and 31 inspiring authors share powerful stories of women who have transformed adversity into strength. Blending personal journeys with practical strategies, this book empowers readers to rise with confidence and resilience. A compelling guide for growth and self-discovery, it reminds every woman that no matter the challenge, she holds the power to grow stronger.

amazon.com   **SHOP NOW**   SHE RISES STUDIOS

SHE RISES
S T U D I O S

*U*NLEASH YOUR STORY
BECOME A PUBLISHED AUTHOR!

Have you ever dreamed of sharing your wisdom, experience, or passion with the world? **Now is your time!**

Publishing a book isn't just about writing—it's about **establishing your authority, inspiring others, and creating a lasting legac**y. Plus, with the **$138.5 billion book industry** booming, there's never been a better moment to step into the spotlight.

At **SRS Publishing**, we don't just publish books—we **elevate voices, empower authors, and create change-makers**. Our mission is to help women break barriers, amplify their stories, and thrive in the publishing world. Whether you're an entrepreneur, thought leader, or storyteller at heart, **we're here to guide you every step of the way.**

JOIN THE FASTEST-GROWING PUBLISHING HOUSE FOR WOMEN IN THE USA.

READY TO TURN YOUR DREAM INTO REALITY?

 www.SheRisesStudios.com | *contact@sherisesstudios.com*